When GOD'S VOICE *is* HEARD

The POWER of preaching

John Stott, J. I. Packer, D. A. Carson,
Frank J. Retief & others

Editors:
Christopher Green & David Jackman

Inter-Varsity Press

INTER-VARSITY PRESS
38 De Montfort Street, Leicester LE1 7GP, England
Email: ivp@uccf.org.uk
Website: www.ivpbooks.com

First published 1995
Reprinted 1996, 1997
New edition 2003

British Library Cataloguing in Publication Data
A catalogue record for this book is available from the British Library.

ISBN 0-85111-284-6

Set in Ehrhardt
Typeset in Great Britain by Parker Typesetting Service, Leicester
Printed in Great Britain by Creative Print and Design (Wales), Ebbw Vale

Inter-Varsity Press is the publishing division of the Universities and Colleges Christian Fellowship (formerly the Inter-Varsity Fellowship), a student movement linking Christian Unions in universities and colleges throughout Great Britain, and a member movement of the International Fellowship of Evangelical Students. For information about local and national activities write to UCCF, 38 De Montfort Street, Leicester LE1 7GP, email us at email@uccf.org.uk, or visit the UCCF website at www.uccf.org.uk.

When GOD'S VOICE *is* HEARD

Contents

III

List of contributors

John Stott, Rector Emeritus, All Souls Church, Langham Place, London, and President of the London Institute for Contemporary Christianity.

Christopher Green, Vice-Principal of Oak Hill Theological College, and formerly Minister of Emmanuel Church, Surbiton, and Study Assistant to Dick Lucas.

Peter Adam, Principal of Ridley College, Melbourne, Australia.

John Woodhouse, Principal of Moore Theological College, Sydney, Australia.

Peter F. Jensen, Archbishop of Sydney, Australia, and formerly Principal of Moore Theological College, Sydney.

Sinclair B. Ferguson, Minister of St George's Tron, Glasgow, and Visiting Professor of Systematic Theology, Westminster Theological Seminary, Philadelphia, USA.

J. I. Packer, Board of Governors Professor of Theology, Regent College, Vancouver, Canada.

Edmund P. Clowney, Emeritus Professor of Practical Theology, Westminster Theological Seminary, Philadelphia, USA, and Westminster Theological Seminary, Escondido, California, USA.

Frank J. Retief, Cape Area Bishop, and Rector of St James' (Church of England in South Africa), Kenilworth, Cape Town, South Africa.

Philip D. Jensen, Rector of St Matthias' Church, Sydney, Australia.

D. A. Carson, Research Professor of New Testament, Trinity Evangelical Divinity School, Deerfield, Illinois, USA.

John Chapman, formerly Director for Evangelism, Sydney Diocese, Australia.

David Jackman, Director of the Cornhill Training Course, London.

Foreword

Half a century's friendship with Dick Lucas has been for me an affirming, liberating and enriching experience. In outline our lives have been similar. Both of us were influenced by 'Bash', both went to Trinity College, Cambridge, and on to Ridley Hall, both were ordained into the Church of England's pastoral ministry, and both became rectors of large London churches. Yet I was about five years ahead of him and have been able to watch and appreciate his ministry at first hand. He has been remarkably successful in combining characteristics which in others are often kept apart.

My first example is relevance and faithfulness. It would not be inaccurate to represent Dick as having the Bible in one hand and the *Financial Times* in the other. If ever a man has found his niche, that man is Dick Lucas. City magnates trust him. He understands their world. He feels for them in their pressures and temptations. And in all his preaching he searches for appropriate application. Never at the expense of faithfulness, however. He believes that God's Word is timeless as well as timely, and he perseveres in his conscientious study of the text until, as he sometimes says, he has 'cracked' it!

He is also a man of culture, a lover of good literature and painting, and a student of the human scene; and has been endowed with a keen, enquiring mind. At the same time, he is pre-eminently (as John Wesley described himself) a person 'of one book, and that book the Bible'. He steadfastly refuses to be distracted from his study and exposition of it by administrative chores, committee work or church bureaucracy. His appointment as a Prebendary of St Paul's Cathedral made his friends smile; the tribute was well deserved but ill suited. He finely exemplifies the priorities of the apostles who determined to devote themselves 'to prayer and the ministry of the word'. I do not mean by this, however, that he neglected necessary duties. For example, his social conscience is seen in his concern for the conversion and rehabilitation of those who used to be called 'Borstal boys' in London's East End, and with his elder brother John he was for many years exemplary in his care of his ageing mother until she died.

If there is anything irrepressible about Dick it is his uproarious sense of humour. Nobody can claim to know him who has not seen him laughing at his own jokes and impersonations, convulsed by a favourite Saki short story, or reduced to helplessness by P. G. Wodehouse's description of a bishop under the influence of large doses of 'Mulliner's Buck-U-Upo'. He loves to mock the pretensions of ecclesiastical bigwigs and to prick the bubbles of human pomposity, not least in the 'rich young rulers' of the City.

Yet he is deadly serious about the gospel. Humour has an important place in the pulpit, especially when the preacher is laughing at himself and the foibles of human behaviour. But it has no place when the eternal issues of life and death, heaven and hell, are being handled. At these times laughter is entirely out of place, as is exhibitionism at all times. I thank God that Dick Lucas, whose only ambition is to see expository preaching enthroned in the world's pulpits, is consistently self-effacing in style, unswerving in purpose, and uncompromising in content. I count it a privilege to be his friend and to salute him on his seventieth birthday.

Easter 1994   *John Stott*

Preaching that shapes a ministry

Dick Lucas and St Helen's, Bishopsgate

Christopher Green

The City of London is packed with empty and redundant churches. Some pre-date the Great Fire in 1666, but most were built as replacements for those that were burnt, so that the seething population might have a place to worship. Now there is barely any resident population at all, and the bankers, accountants, traders and messengers who crowd the Square Mile in the week leave the place deserted by the weekend. The appointments of clergy to City churches are often to allow them a wider work elsewhere, or as semi-retirement posts.

In the heart of the City is a great exception. Every Tuesday hundreds of City workers give up their lunchtime to listen to a sermon. In the evenings another set of hundreds of young people meet to study Mark's gospel and Romans. On Sundays the church is packed with young families and students, drawn by a clear explanation of the Bible. St Helen's Church, led by Dick Lucas, is a rare phenomenon: a large and growing church in a hard and secular environment. The Church of England is closing church buildings in the City, but St Helen's is at the end of a building project to expand its seating capacity to 1,000. This reversal of a trend requires explanation.

Dick is celebrating his seventieth birthday, and it seems appropriate to honour him and his ministry with this book. It is not a book about him, for that would focus the attention on quite the wrong place and he would hate it. Indeed, he has banned histories of St Helen's in the past. Instead it is a book about his greatest passion, the preaching of the Bible. All the other contributors have written on their areas of experience in relation to the task of explaining God's Word. This chapter, though, uses St Helen's as a test case, to see how a ministry which is governed by a desire to teach God's Word has been shaped to achieve that end, how it has equipped others for their God-given ministries, and how it has become one that changes thousands of lives even in a post-modern society at the end of the twentieth century.

One of Dick's delights as a boy was the little metal puzzles that come in Christmas crackers; a twist of the puzzle one way and a jerk of the wrist the other, and a tangle of metalwork becomes clearly resolved into its simple parts. In many ways, Dick's approach to the Bible is much the same. He will return to the same passage, time and again, trying to understand it better, looking for the surprises, observing it, twisting it round until the puzzle is solved and the passage falls cleanly apart. Watching him handle a passage, you would think it is simple – until you try it, and realize it is much harder than it looks. That constant delight in Scripture that leads him to try over again, to find a new way and a fresh angle, is what has led people to stay under his teaching ministry, and learn how he teaches, over many years.

The roots of a ministry

Dick Lucas came to a large and mostly empty St Helen's in 1961. He had been in the Royal Navy during the war and then trained for the ministry in Cambridge. This had led to a curacy at St Nicholas' Church in Sevenoaks, a well-established evangelical church, and then to work for the Church Pastoral Aid Society.

But (as for so many leaders of his generation), the single most important figure in his early years was the deeply loved 'Bash', E. H. Nash, who ran a series of summer holidays for young public-school boys where they could hear and respond to the gospel and then be brought to full Christian maturity. Michael Green, John Stott and David Watson were among the many Christian leaders who learned the lessons of devotion to Christ and his work summer by summer at Iwerne Minster. It was in this environment that Dick had first become a Christian and then learned how to be a useful Christian worker. 'Bash' maintained a long and caring relationship with his 'campers'; many years later he would be seen slipping into the back of a meeting where one of them was preaching, and would write to them subsequently, giving wise, if not always welcome, advice. This was invaluable to Dick as he was becoming known as a well-proven leader of student missions in universities, and beginning to make his name in a wider circle.

In the City a small group of businessmen had been praying regularly each Monday lunchtime for seven years, seeking God's guidance for the way to spread the gospel in their workplace. They invited Dick to give a series of four lunchtime addresses in St Mary Abchurch. About a hundred men came. Across the City one of the old livery guilds, the Merchant Taylors, was considering whom to invite to become Rector of their unusually roomy medieval church. They heard about Dick's series. 'Is it true, Mr Lucas, that you are filling St Mary Abchurch? Then you had better come and fill St Helen's.'

That inauspicious beginning contained many of the seeds of all the subsequent work. It was founded on the basis of praying laymen, who wanted to hear the Bible taught – and that was what they got. Without that core of men, Dick's coming to the City would have been an irrelevance; but with it he could be sure that there was a need and a support. On the back of it, and praying together, they could build a work to reach out to the surrounding world. The immediate area was small; someone has said that if you served a tennis ball from St Helen's you would hit the Baltic Exchange; a boundary six would hit the Lloyd's building, and a good drive off a tee would break a window in the Stock Exchange. But that small area is the most precious office space in London, and it was to the men – and the City workers in those days were almost universally men – who worked in those offices that Dick's ministry was directed. Breaking all traditions, he centred not on the Sunday but on the midweek work, for that was when the City was busy. Ignoring the Anglican liturgy, the service began with a hymn, a Bible reading and a prayer, and then went straight into a twenty-two-minute sermon, timed exactly to leave room for people to eat lunch and return to their desks in time.

Still today those who occupy that slot in Dick's absences have to fulfil that tight time control. It looks so easy until it is tried, and then Dick's mastery of his task becomes clear. God raised up a man to do a unique work. The people who come midweek are of course in many places on Sundays, and that has meant that hundreds of smaller fellowships have felt the benefit of first-rate Bible teaching without losing their members to an empire-building megachurch.

It flourished, and the Tuesday lunchtime services came to need two sittings. It grew some small study ('Partnership') breakfasts to heighten the personal discipling, and added a junior partner on Thursday lunchtimes, Channel Five, to reach a new generation of City workers. Once again the pattern of constant evolution and change, reappraisal and doing it differently becomes clear. One of Dick's greatest assets is the way he gets bored so quickly! Essentially the ministry development at St Helen's has been a classic piece of pioneer mission, reaching to the unchurched groups in a clearly defined area.

Riding the wave of the unexpected

For the staff who have joined Dick over the years, his pioneer mentality has proved both a refreshing environment and a constant hurdle. No-one who has worked closely with him has ever enjoyed a fixed job description, but the wise ones know that, and enjoy riding the wave of the unexpected. There have been no regular staff meetings, although there have been stimulating study mornings with outside speakers. No-one who has preached has ever received a regular and detailed analysis of the sermon. 'It was', said one man reflecting on his time at St Helen's, 'like being allowed to work in Rembrandt's studio, but without Rembrandt commenting on your work. On the other hand, you were able to watch Rembrandt at *his* work.' That is, indeed, the key. He bounces his ideas round with his colleagues, boxing with the passage, trying the fresh ideas and new insights until he is convinced about what he thinks. It is valuable to see the final results of his work, but much more valuable to see the questions he asks as he wrestles with a passage.

Occasionally Dick's improvisatory style could backfire, as when both Jonathan Fletcher and Jim Spence turned up on a Sunday expecting to preach. On another Sunday, when Jonathan was in the south of France, Jim was at St Helen's conference centre in Surrey, and no-one knew where Dick was. Someone hurriedly led a service from scratch, and Steve James dug into the tape library for one of Dick's old sermons. The whole episode left Dick quite unperturbed. 'It's really very surprising it hasn't happened before,' he said. 'It will teach people how badly they need us.' When he was told that actually the service had been a great success and people had enjoyed it, he tried a different tack: 'In that case we must try it again.' Dick usually wins.

Read, Mark, Learn

St Helen's was growing by the mid-seventies, and lots of younger people, who were new Christians, needed to be taught further. Staff members had come and gone: Ian Barclay had strengthened the preaching team, Bob Howarth had provided warmth and a sense of family, and St Helen's was an enjoyable place to be. The rich humour spilt into many areas of the church life, which included such memorable New Year treats as a performance of *Trial by Jury* with Dick as a particularly outrageous Judge.

Yet the congregations were often too large for people to feel they belonged, and so a new concept needed to be developed. Quoting an Anglican prayer for God to teach us from the Bible, it was to be called 'Read, Mark, Learn' (RML). In some ways the idea was not new at all, since every generation of thriving churches has to discover the need for a small-group network. RML, as it was known, began life as a series of talks by Dick from Mark's gospel. Gradually, this developed into a one-year pattern of Bible studies: the groups meet, with one group responsible for the cooking; this fosters a sense of belonging and purpose. They study a passage; this is followed by a talk on some aspect of Christian living, and then by a preparation session for those leading the Bible study the following week. The quality is assured, because staff members teach the group leaders, and the group leaders will themselves have been through RML in previous years. There is a social programme as well, and the whole system is characterized by people enjoying themselves hugely. Mark's gospel is now year one of RML, and year two offers a choice of studying either Romans or an overview of the whole Bible. The principle of teaching the Bible-study leaders before they themselves lead is followed through, and there are large workbooks for group leaders and members for all three courses.

It can become cerebral, and certainly some people have found that the emphasis on understanding a given interpretation has meant that other genuine insights have been lost and that the groups are too task-driven without enough sense of fellowship. Yet RML has given young people both a tool that they themselves can use, and the ability to handle the Bible with confidence. And it has done so in the context of a place where they belonged and were needed. In themselves those factors might begin to explain why, in the late seventies, the evening service suddenly doubled in size, and then doubled again. The services were informal and casual, with not a dog collar or cassock in sight, and had a bright, contemporary feel. So even today, in the City, in a parish where no-one but Dick and a night watchman live, hundreds of students sit under solid Bible teaching, week after week.

Preaching conferences

Over the years Dick has had many ideas. Many have vanished into obscurity as soon as reality hit, and a few have been tried and have not survived; but one or two have been of remarkable importance. The generations of younger preachers who claim him as their model have had no written work which they could draw upon, and although many could imitate the voice, no-one could ever imitate the preaching style. The deep influence Dick has exercised among future pastors and teachers springs almost completely from the elegantly simple idea of the expository preaching conferences.

In 1981 Dick began to be aware that the younger clergy were saying that they had never been taught how to expound the Bible. This was a major deficiency which, if left unchecked, would wreak havoc in the future. Jonathan Fletcher invited forty-five people to Fairmile Court, the church's conference centre in Surrey, and forty-one people came. They took it in turns to speak on the passages that Dick had set beforehand. Every one of them gave what Dick called 'a camp talk': they had been taught to teach the Bible on the same camps Dick himself had been on, and they all presented basic gospel outlines that were virtually identical to one another. Every single one had misread the passage.

Dick's response was to set up an annual preaching conference at which the participants would come with their prepared talks, listen to one another, and slowly learn the hard way how to hear Scripture 'right', in Dick's phrase. Now those lessons from Rembrandt's studio would become available to a wider audience, and they too would learn how Dick questions a passage. As the poverty of preaching became clear, it became obvious that other issues in church leadership would need to be addressed as well. Dick had exploded the myth that evangelicals were firm on Scripture, and now Phillip Jensen from Sydney came to speak. He showed how far evangelicals had drifted from their historical roots. For most of those attending, it was their first exposure to this radical Australian as he handed them back their Reformation (and deeply Anglican) theology, and taught them the necessity of putting Scripture first over their traditions. Following the success of Phillip's visit, it became the custom to invite an outsider to speak off the record.

As the conference grew, and then spawned a 'newcomers' conference', the basic lessons were hammered home: preach the text and not a theological framework, look for the surprises in the passage, try to find the main idea of a book (what Dick calls 'the melodic line'), and above all, simple observation. 'Take the passage back to its original hearers,' he would say. 'Travel to Corinth' – a principle named after the discovery that 1 Corinthians 13, in the context of the letter, is actually a severe reprimand. Time and again the speaker would fall into some elephant trap or other, by failing to look hard enough at the text. 'Well, that was very interesting, brother,' Dick said to one hapless expositor. 'Now, can anyone tell me what the passage really means?' As usual, despite the relentless critiques of expositions, there was massive good humour: Dick would read P. G. Wodehouse ('The Great Sermon Handicap' being a frequently requested treat), or an entire lecture room would weep with laughter as he peered out from behind the curtains to show the pointlessness of clergy vestments. ('Do I look more dignified now? Do I?')

The roots of all this lay far back, in Dick's experiences of the officers' rooms at 'Bash's' camps, where the talks and activities of the previous day were thoroughly reviewed in order to teach the younger men how to do a task before they were ever entrusted with one. Dick raised this principle to a new level. Experienced preachers from the country's largest churches would come, fully expecting that material which would be quite acceptable in their home environment would fail the master's eye. One preacher would have put in too much application. 'Too many vegetables on the plate,' said Dick, sternly. Another would bluff, vainly trying to hide his lack of preparation. 'What's your main point, in one sentence?' was the usual question to expose that failure.

There have been flaws in this system. Sometimes an emphasis on 'getting it right' has led the younger preachers to be over-intellectual, and to preach above the heads of an ordinary church. One sometimes meets those who never listen to a sermon to hear God speak, but only to observe a theorist. Of course, no-one ever 'gets it right' completely, and Dick is the principal example of that, never keeping his sermons, but always refining them, constantly tuning his approach to get it closer to the Bible's. Familiar hands knew that when Dick promised to speak on what he called 'treasures old', he meant that he was going to have another go at a passage on which they had heard him many times before, but precisely because of that he would be worth hearing. The conferences can be tough at times, and not everyone enjoyed the rather hearty atmosphere. Some people came and went without ever having opened their mouths. Some people learned abrasiveness at the expense of love. But the real end result is wave after wave of younger ministers who will not rest satisfied with their initial thoughts, but will work hard, hour after hour, to sit under God's Word, and to enable other people to become more godly. All over the country there are small groups of ministers who meet month by month to 'crit' one another's sermons and keep each other sharp. One of the most valuable lessons has been that the essentially lonely task of the preacher has become more of a team effort, each one encouraging the other.

The Proclamation Trust

By 1986 Dick had been at St Helen's for twenty-five years, but it was clear that this was not a time for slowing down or starting to retire. His anniversary was marked by the start of a wholly new venture. Ronald Wilcox, who had known Dick from the earliest days at St Helen's and had been the first face many saw as they entered for a Tuesday lunchtime service, crystallized with Dick the formation of the Proclamation Trust. (Ronnie Wilcox died as this book was in preparation. He will be fondly missed.) St Helen's had been loyally carrying the burden of organizing the preaching conferences. Now, a firm financial base would mean that the whole organization could move up a gear. Dick would have a full-time staff worker whose sole task was to support him as he increasingly left the running of St Helen's in the hands of others. By this time his regular church commitments were only to his beloved Tuesday lunchtimes, although he preached often on Sundays. He found himself travelling overseas, speaking at conferences and leading preachers' workshops all over the world. On his own this would have been impossible, for he had never even had a full-time personal secretary (although the church office, of course, was fully staffed); he wrote his letters in longhand and did not even have a filing system. He relied instead on his excellent – if suspiciously selective – memory.

The Evangelical Ministry Assembly

The Proclamation Trust could now realize another idea: the Evangelical Ministry Assembly (EMA). In the past, Anglican evangelical ministers had attended an annual convention in London called the Islington Conference, but this had died. There was no longer any regular place for clergy to hear good speakers address the issues affecting ministry. Dick saw this as an urgent need. Equally urgent was the need to tackle the sad division between Anglican and Free Church ministers. Dick had long seen that unity in the gospel was real unity, and that only human traditions were holding brothers and sisters at arm's length. He also saw that the hand of friendship should be extended by Anglicans first, because it was the public face of the Church of England which had given most offence. Back in 1966 Martyn Lloyd-Jones had delivered an impassioned plea for gospel men to leave the Church of England and form a new evangelical grouping, and John Stott had called them to remain and work to regain and reform the denomination. It is still too early to say whether it was ever true that only one of those strategies was right. But one of the side-effects of the parting of the ways (a side-effect neither man intended) was a division between evangelicals that caused decades of mistrust. Now, with the Evangelical Ministry Assembly, it might be possible to repair some bridges of fellowship. As the scale of the conference outgrew St Helen's, it found a new home in Central Hall, Westminster, the very place where the division occurred.

Once again, God's hand was on Dick's brainchild and the conference has proved a major part of the evangelical year. Speakers are flown in from around the world – most of the other contributors to this volume have been on the EMA platform – and a number of the addresses have been of an importance that will be fully seen only in the decades to come. Phillip Jensen's addresses on ministry and church revolutionized people literally overnight, and have earned them an almost cult status among ministers in training. Preachers have heard some of the finest expositors in the world, and have set their own sights higher. They have been challenged on their own weaknesses as Christians, strengthened by their fellowship, and moved by the wonder of the privilege of being God's co-workers. They have gone home driven by a renewed desire to labour even harder in the Lord's vineyard. It is fitting that this book, aimed at the preacher, written in honour of a master preacher, should be launched from the platform of the EMA.

Cornhill

From a number of viewpoints Dick had been observing for himself the training that young ministers were offered, and he had not been impressed. It seemed that none of the older denominations was able to offer a course which left students thrilled by the Bible and equipped to teach it in the churches. In fact, some of the colleges were notorious for undermining the faith of their students. Once again an idea began to form, this time that it should be possible to bypass the training colleges with their academic agenda and produce preachers who would be able to fill the pulpits of churches. He knew that it could be done; he had seen what the Sydney evangelicals were achieving at Moore College. The Australian ethic of pragmatism was beginning to influence him. Why should we have to put up with the wrong kind of training when we could do something better? The idea was shared by David Jackman, who had developed a training element in his time at Above Bar Church in Southampton, and was considering how to include a number of people from other churches and give them a basis for the pastorate.

The Proclamation Trust seemed the ideal sponsoring body, and Dick and David between them could manage most of the lecturing. The only realistic venue would be central London, because each of the students would have to fulfil church-related assignments and it would be hard to find a suitably large number of supportive churches anywhere else in the country. So David and Heather Jackman left Southampton to move to London. The only possible site would have to be yet another City church, and by this time St Peter's Church on Cornhill, near St Helen's, became vacant during the week. It was a spacious and light Wren building which needed to have considerable work done to the floor, but which would provide a suitable lecture space, a library and a study for David, together with a new office for the Proclamation Trust.

The plan for the Cornhill Training Course, as it was called, was simple. The only entry qualification was that the person should have a proven record as a preacher, at however early a stage, and should desire to improve that gift. The course would require no written assignments or reading beyond what was needed to preach in a placement church and to participate in the sermon classes on Friday afternoons. In addition to Dick and David, there was to be a wide range of visiting lecturers to cover all aspects of handling and teaching the Bible. The first year's students knew that they were guinea-pigs, and had tremendous fun in the process. There were, and still are, no final-term examinations: the final results could be measured only by the difference in their preaching. The same has been true of the students of subsequent years. They have come from a wide range of backgrounds, and from a growing international pool. Yet the joint determination to 'find the melodic line' of a book, under Dick's inspiration, has produced an impressive legacy of keen and equipped younger ministers.

Opening up his Rembrandt studio meant that as Dick prepared a new set of lectures (perhaps the 'Expositions for Expositors', which drew ministers from all over London on a weekday morning), another circle of younger preachers would watch him at work, and learn. One of the first year's graduates found that he was speaking in a church where D. A. Carson was in the congregation. Carson was unsurprised to hear that the young man had been to Cornhill; there was, he said, 'a cutting edge' to the sermon.

Enduring hardship

On Friday 10 April 1992, Dick was expecting some friends for supper who had to cancel at the last minute. With an unexpected evening free, he went to bed early with a P. G. Wodehouse novel. Because hardly anyone lives in the City, its Friday evenings are usually quiet, most of the workers preferring to go home rather than to the wine bars. This Friday, though, was the day after a General Election, and the City was full of happy Conservatives celebrating a fourth term of government and a first victory for John Major. Inside St Helen's, an organist was rehearsing for a wedding the next day, and the finishing touches were being made to the flower arrangements.

At 9.25pm a 100 lb terrorist bomb exploded 50 yards away from Dick's Rectory. It had been planted by the IRA outside the Baltic Exchange, the centre of the City's shipping market. The aim was presumably to damage the City's international reputation and also to mark the election in a particularly macabre way. The force rocked the twenty-seven-storey Commercial Union building and shattered almost every window for a quarter of a mile. The City was plunged into darkness as viciously sharp glass fragments rained down from the tall office buildings. The van which was used for the bomb completely disintegrated in the blast, leaving a crater 10 feet deep. Its engine was found on the eighth storey of a bank.

Casualties were few but tragic: three people died, including a fifteen-year-old girl, and ninety-seven people were injured. The packed bars were mostly underground, and the people in them were frightened but safe. A taxi driver left his car and ran, leaving the door wide open behind him. An electrician who was working in the basement of the Commercial Union building was convinced that his faulty wiring had blown a fuse that had exploded all over the City, and only the newspapers the next day convinced him that he was not to blame.

Dick himself had been saved only by being in his bedroom, on the opposite side of the building to the bomb. The shock waves had dislodged his front door and door-frame from the surrounding wall. The windows in his kitchen and living-room imploded with sickening force, and fragmented into thousands of deadly glass shards which pierced the walls and the furniture to a terrifying depth. The many photographs of friends, which were on the kitchen walls, were shredded. The chairs and tables were scarred and ripped. His car, which had faced the full force of the bomb, was twisted and destroyed beyond recognition. Guessing that this was a terrorist attack, Dick set off to find the people who had been working in the church. They were cut, but not seriously hurt. Had the bomb gone off the previous evening, there would have been carnage; the Read, Mark, Learn students would have been pouring out of St Andrew's (a building it had adapted) into the street where the bomb exploded.

As the chaos of that night and the next few days began to subside, it became clear that the damage to the buildings and ministry was severe. By detonating a bomb so close to St Helen's, the IRA had deprived the church of all its usable buildings. There was nowhere to meet for the Tuesday and Sunday services, and nowhere to house Read, Mark, Learn (St Andrew's also having suffered serious bomb damage). There was no office space, study space or seminar rooms. The only building that could be used in that central block was the tiny St Ethelburga Bishopsgate, the smallest church in the City of London. It had a vestry, which was rapidly turned into an emergency office, but the main body of the building was out of use because restoration work was in progress.

While the church and the staff came to terms with what had happened, Dick himself was on top form. His home had been destroyed, but he moved into a small flat. He delighted in telling the City business people that although the building may have been wrecked, the gospel was unaffected. 'John Betjeman used to say that Great St Helen's was notable for only two things,' he said, 'bad Victorian glass and extreme evangelicalism. At least the extreme evangelicalism is intact.' It was perhaps good for his peace of mind that he had to visit the States almost immediately for a preaching and lecturing tour. On his return the Tuesday lunchtime services recommenced, and packed the magnificent Guildhall.

To a superficial onlooker, the church would seem to have recovered quickly. The Sunday morning services transferred to St Peter's, Cornhill, where, instead of feeling slightly lost in a large building, they filled a smaller space comfortably. RML had to stop providing hot meals, but they too met in St Peter's. The Tuesday lunchtime services moved to a nearby church, St Botolph without Bishopsgate, which also proved a temporary home for Sunday evening. A nearby office building, Plantation House, provided ideal space for all the staff; for the first time they had modern, spacious offices, and they loved it. The initial spirit was very positive, with everyone coping well, and saying to one another that 'at least it was only the building and not the church that was bombed'.

This buoyant mood was tempered over time as the reality of how long it would take to repair the buildings, and how much it would cost, began to dawn. Buildings may not be the church, but they are a great asset to a church. Before the bomb the church had been gearing up to a mission week, and now they found it hard to run such an event without a clear central venue. The Tuesday lunchtimes began to suffer too, as people in a hurry to get back to their offices could no longer depend on knowing where it would happen and whether their lunch would be supplied.

Within nine months the situation had stabilized, and architects' plans were being drawn up. The office records and equipment had been salvaged or replaced. The precious library of preaching and lecture tapes had taken the full impact of the explosion, but had been protected by the solid medieval walls, and had only to be moved and dusted. But Dick Lucas himself had taken a heavy toll over the past year. In addition to the disruption, he had undergone some routine surgery, and had lost his much-loved mother. The stresses of his public ministry were high, as both the EMA and the autumn lectures were drawing larger numbers of ministers. Wisely, he decided that he could not repeat the 'Expositions for Expositors' of the preceding autumns, for he had no time to do the kind of preparation that had been required for his Romans or 1 Corinthians lectures. Instead, he gave himself time to concentrate on his new material for the Cornhill Training Course. Despite all expectations, the shape of the ministry at St Helen's had been surprisingly unaffected by the terrorists' attack.

But then came a harder blow. The quiet Saturday morning of 24 April 1993 was the timing for a second IRA car bomb: one ton of high explosive detonated by 10 lbs of Semtex.

Again the aim was to disrupt London's financial work and reputation. But there were other casualties too. A press photographer was killed and forty people were injured. The bomb site was the Hong Kong and Shanghai Bank, which had been damaged in the previous explosion. But once more St Helen's was an indirect target. The little church of St Ethelburga's, earmarked to be the home of the Discovering Christianity course, and the temporary office after the first bomb, was alongside the explosion and was completely destroyed. Nothing remained but a rear wall. The foundations of St Helen's, which had been rocked by the first bomb, were rocked once again. Precious time had been spent in surveying the building before the architects could start work; now that tedious and expensive process had to start all over again. But much more serious for the ministry was the fact that St Botolph's, the building which had become the new venue for both Tuesday and Sunday evenings, was rendered completely unusable.

Morale after the first bomb had been surprisingly high, as people had taken to a challenge. Now they were faced with the task once more, and they were sober. The first Sunday evening service was held in the office in Plantation House. It was a full room, but the mood was nowhere near as cheerful as after the first explosion. It was beginning to dawn on the church staff and members that arrangements which had been made on the understanding that they were temporary were going to have to be semi-permanent. Buildings may not be the church, but the lack of them was beginning to hinder the church in major ways. Alternative venues were again found, and most of the activity centred around St Peter's. RML was based there, as was the central prayer meeting and the Sunday services. In fact, a new phase was initiated because the evening congregation was too large for its new home and had to split into two. As the church struggled to regain its composure, there were nervous jokes about a third bomb.

As I write, there has not been one, and the work of teaching the Bible is continuing on its firm footing. St Andrew's Undershaft is again in use, providing the extra seats lacking before, and with a bright feel for its interior. St Helen's is being restored and, after a long battle with various historically minded groups, made more useful for the work in the next century. This is no time to look back. And the plan is that over the entrance to the restored St Helen's Jesus' words will remind anyone who comes of the indestructible heart of the ministry that builds into eternity: 'Heaven and earth may pass away, but my words will never pass away.'

I

2

The preacher and the sufficient Word

Presuppositions of biblical preaching

Peter Adam

Question: Are you persuaded that the Holy Scriptures contain sufficiently all doctrine required of necessity for eternal salvation, through faith in Jesus Christ? And are you determined out of the same Holy Scriptures to instruct the people committed to your charge; and to teach or maintain nothing as required of necessity to eternal salvation, but that which you shall be persuaded may be concluded and proved by the same?

Answer: I am so persuaded and have so determined, by God's grace.[1]

I am personally very grateful for the ministry of Dick Lucas at St Helen's, Bishopsgate. When I was a student at King's College, London, studying New Testament under Professor C. F. Evans in the early 1970s, I was always greatly encouraged by the faithful preaching of the Word at St Helen's. At the time I had Sunday preaching responsibilities at St George the Martyr, Queen's Square, and at Christ Church,

Woburn Square. On my free Sundays and often on a Tuesday I would wend my way to St Helen's and benefit from the Bible plainly taught.

Dick Lucas represents part of the great resurgence of Reformed expository preaching that has taken place in Great Britain after the Second World War. This resurgence was represented by Martyn Lloyd-Jones at Westminster Chapel, John Stott at All Souls, Langham Place, Dick Lucas at St Helen's, and William Still in Aberdeen. As far as I can work out, these were independent attempts to reassert the centrality and sufficiency of Scripture in the preaching of the church; they reflected the great expository preaching of Calvin in Geneva, and of Augustine and John Chrysostom in the early church.

It is interesting to note that this expository preaching tradition, that of preaching through books of the Bible, died out in the early church because of the growing ignorance of the clergy, the increasing liturgical complexity of the services, and the need for topical preaching to deal with contemporary theological issues.[2]

What these twentieth-century preachers have had in common is a commitment to treat the Bible as if it were indeed the sufficient Word of God, the belief that by explaining it and applying it to their congregations they were achieving God's purposes, and a Reformed understanding of Scripture and the gospel. Their common commitment to the sufficiency of Scripture has meant that they have been impatient of any traditions added by human authority. In this sense their preaching was truly ecumenical, in that it depended on that which all Christians have in common, the Holy Scriptures.

The sufficiency of Scripture

The doctrine of the sufficiency of Scripture is explained clearly in the words of Henry Bullinger in his second sermon on the Word of God.

> Now because I have said that the Word of God is revealed, to the intent that it may fully instruct us in the ways of God and our salvation; I will in a few words declare unto you, dearly beloved, that in the Word of God, delivered to us by the prophets and apostles, is abundantly contained the whole effect of godliness, and what things soever are available to the leading of our lives rightly well and holily. For, verily, it must needs be, that *that doctrine is full, and in all points perfect, to which nothing ought either to be added, or else to be taken away* . . . Ye have, brethren, an evident testimony of *the fullness of the Word of God*, ye have *a doctrine absolutely perfect in all points.*[3]

Bullinger is asserting that the Bible is the sufficient Word of God, that is, that it includes everything that God wishes to say to human beings. From this doctrine of the sufficiency of the Bible it follows that Christian gospel ministry involves explaining, preaching, applying and interpreting this sufficient Word so that people may be converted and congregations may be built up in faith, godliness and usefulness.

The doctrine of the sufficiency of Scripture is that the Bible consists of the preserved written words of God, and that this book is sufficient revelation to show us salvation in Jesus Christ, and all other information and instruction to lead godly lives as the people of God. It asserts that God's revelation in Jesus Christ, as interpreted in the Old and New Testaments, is a sufficient interpretation; that it does not need further revelation or interpretation to make it complete. It asserts that in Jesus Christ God achieved his revelatory purposes, and that the Bible contains sufficient works, signs and words for us to understand that revelation. It asserts that this sufficiency does not need to be complemented by tradition or reason, that Scripture is universally sufficient for all people and for all time until the return of Christ, and that Scripture is the sufficient revelation to achieve the corporate maturity of God's people in any age.

Does the doctrine of the sufficiency of Scripture imply that *my* understanding of the Bible is infallible, or that *I* understand Scripture sufficiently? No, it makes no such promise, but it encourages me to work hard at understanding and using Scripture, believing that through it God provides his complete revelation for this age. I will need the help of others to understand the Bible rightly, for I believe in a God-given Bible-sufficiency, and not self-sufficiency.

Does the doctrine of the sufficiency of Scripture imply that we have no need of teachers and preachers in the church? (This view is often expressed by clergy when they say that their hope in ministry is to do themselves out of a job, and by lay people who believe that they have no need of teachers, for the Bible itself is sufficient for them.) No, for the Bible itself tells us of our need of overseers or elders who are able to teach, who 'encourage . . . by sound doctrine' and 'refute those who oppose it' (Tit. 1:9). A congregation which does not have this ministry is 'left unfinished' (Tit. 1:5). Elsewhere these elders are described as 'leaders . . . who spoke the word of God' . . . those who 'keep watch over you as men who must give an account' (Heb. 13:7, 17). And Paul instructs these elders: 'Keep watch over yourselves and all the flock of which the Holy Spirit has made you overseers. Be shepherds of the church of God, which he bought with his own blood' (Acts 20:28).

So Calvin dismisses those who think 'that they can profit enough from private reading and meditation; hence they despise public

assemblies and deem preaching superfluous'.[4] For the God who gave us
the Bible also gives us teachers and preachers: this God does to show
his regard for us in making humans his mouthpiece, to teach us
humility in that we have to receive his words 'when a puny man risen
from the dust speaks in God's name', and because in giving and
receiving of pastor and congregation mutual love is increased.[5] So also
Calvin teaches that God not only accommodates himself to us in his
revelation in giving us the Bible in which he speaks at our level, but
also accommodates to us in giving us teachers and preachers: in them
he 'chews our morsels for us that we might digest them the better',[6]
that is, he makes Scripture more understandable and more easily
received or digested. And preachers add passion, because without it we
will be slow to respond to God's words: 'the doctrine of itself can profit
nothing at all unless it be confirmed by exhortations and threats, unless
there be spurs to prick men withall'.[7] For 'if teaching be not helped
with exhortations it is cold and pierces not our hearts'.[8] So we should
not perceive the ministry of teachers and preachers as redundant, but
as part of God's gracious provision for us. Preachers add purpose and
passion to God's written Word!

The insufficient Scripture

The doctrine of the sufficiency of Scripture must be seen in contrast to
those traditions which assert the insufficiency of Scripture either
directly or by implication. They do so by claiming that the Bible needs
to be supplemented by more recent revelation, or corrected by more
recent revelation, or that we need a God-given authorized interpretation which is the key to Scripture, and by which it must be understood.
We can see the doctrine of the insufficiency of Scripture represented in
the following traditions.

The Roman Catholic Church teaches the insufficiency of Scripture by
asserting that the tradition of the church is of equal value and necessity
as the means by which God's voice is heard.

> Sacred Tradition and sacred Scripture, then, are bound
> closely together, and communicate one with another. For
> both of them, flowing out of the same divine wellspring, come
> together in some fashion to form one thing, and move
> towards the same goal. Sacred Scripture is the speech of God
> as it is put down in writing under the breath of the Holy
> Spirit. And Tradition transmits in its entirety the Word of
> God which has been entrusted to the apostles by Christ the
> Lord and the Holy Spirit . . . thus it comes about that the
> Church does not draw her certainty about all revealed truths

from the Holy Scripture alone. Hence both Scripture and Tradition must be accepted and honoured with equal feelings of devotion and reverence. Sacred Tradition and sacred Scripture make up a single sacred deposit of the Word of God which is entrusted to the Church.[9]

The teaching is clear that Scripture by itself is insufficient. But not only is Scripture insufficient by itself; it also needs interpretation. 'But the task of giving an authentic interpretation of the Word of God, whether in its written form or in the form of tradition, has been entrusted to the living teaching office of the Church alone.'[10] So the document asserts that not only do sacred Scripture and sacred tradition form the one deposit of the Word of God, but also that this Word of God needs to be interpreted by the living teaching office of the church.

Quakers and some charismatics alike assert that if Scripture is preserved, it also needs to be complemented and supplemented and completed by the contemporary voice of the Spirit of God within the believer or within the congregation.

Liberal Christians believe that Scripture has to be subject to reason and interpreted by our understanding of what is acceptable in our age.

Some Anglicans continue to assert the need for the threefold authority of Scripture, tradition and reason, though in practice their authority consists of reason making use of aspects of Scripture and tradition where these seem to be helpful.

Sects such as *Christian Science* and the *Church of Jesus Christ of Latter-Day Saints (Mormons)* believe that Scripture is insufficient and needs to be interpreted by more contemporary documents.

Some evangelicals, while asserting the sufficiency of Scripture in theory, show their belief in the insufficiency of Scripture in practice by teaching evangelical traditions rather than Scripture. These evangelical hobby-horses (perfectionism, the higher life, healing, the latest church-growth theory, or merely the theological preoccupations of the preacher) are taught in place of Scripture.

Some forms of liberation theology assert that Scripture can be rightly understood only in the light of the other text, that of our society and world. This transfers an observation (we always read Scripture in a particular historical context) into a theological necessity, in which Scripture provides the words or images, and the teacher's worldview provides the content of those words or images.

The common feature of those who teach the insufficiency of Scripture in theory or in practice is the belief that the Bible is a good start, but that it needs new material to supplement it, and by which we interpret it. We can represent this view in diagram 1. The doctrine of the sufficiency of Scripture can be represented in diagram 2. We must refute the idea that Scripture provides a good basic framework but that full maturity of faith and church life comes from some other source. Fullness of life and faith is found in the Scripture, God's sufficient Word.

Of course, we cannot ignore the problems of knowing how to respond to different parts of Scripture. But it is important to remember that the question of using the Old Testament for Christian living was a question for the earliest Gentile (and Jewish!) Christian communities and is tackled in the New Testament. And the problem of background knowledge (for instance, of the Corinthian letters) is one that we share with the first-century church in Jerusalem or Rome.

The good Reformation principle is that God has given us Scripture to understand Scripture: that the Bible is a self-interpreting book, and so that the key to understanding the Bible is the internal biblical hermeneutic of comparing Scripture with Scripture.

The sufficiency and effectiveness of Scripture

The doctrine that complements the sufficiency of Scripture is that of the efficiency, or effectiveness, of Scripture: that is, that the Bible is not only sufficient to teach us about God but is also effective in doing so. So Bishop Jewel, writing on the Scriptures, says:

> The whole Word of God is pure and holy. No word, no letter, no syllable, no point nor tittle thereof but is written and preserved for thy sake.

He then continues with a series of questions and instructions:

> Art thou a king? Read the Scriptures . . . Art thou a subject? Read the Scriptures . . . Art thou a minister? Read the Scriptures . . . Art thou a father, hast thou children? Read the Scriptures . . . Art thou a child, hast thou a father? Read the Scriptures . . . Hath God blessed thee in wealth? Art thou rich? Read the Scriptures . . . Art thou poor and sufferest scarcity in the world? Read the Scriptures . . . Art thou a merchant? Read the Scriptures. Art thou a usurer? Read the Scriptures. Art thou a fornicator? Read the Scriptures. Art thou a servant? Read the Scriptures. Art thou proud? Read the Scriptures. Art thou in adversity? Read the Scriptures. Art thou a sinner? Hast thou offended God? Read the Scriptures. Dost thou despair of the mercy of God? Read the Scriptures. Art thou going out of this life? Read the Scriptures.[11]

THE PREACHER AND THE SUFFICIENT WORD

1. The insufficiency of Scripture

BC/AD ⟶ 20th/21st centuries

The Bible is a good start	The gap to our day should be filled by:	
	• the teaching and traditions of the church (Catholic)	
	• contemporary personal or corporate revelation (Quaker or charismatic)	
	• reason (liberal)	
	• recent documents which explain the truth (*e.g.* the Book of Mormon)	
	• a new reading of Scripture by the text of today's world	
	• evangelical tradition or reductive simplifications of Scripture	

2. The sufficiency of Scripture

God speaks to us today by the words he spoke long ago

to them   for us

so that Scripture is God's contemporary Word to us today

BC/AD ⟶ 20th/21st centuries

The Bible ⟶ able to make us wise for salvation through faith in Christ Jesus, and to equip us for every good work

Scripture is both sufficient and effective. Because it is sufficient it is effective in God's hand.

Arguments for the sufficiency of Scripture

It is evident that not everyone who claims to be Christian believes in the sufficiency of Scripture. What then are the arguments that we can use to defend this doctrine? There are three main arguments: from *Jesus Christ*, from the nature of *salvation history*, and from *the Bible itself*.

1. Jesus Christ

It is clear that the Bible is a book about Jesus Christ. The Old Testament points forward to Christ and his work; the gospels describe his life on earth, his teaching, his death and his resurrection; and in the Acts, the letters and the book of Revelation we have the general apostolic explanation of the meaning of the coming of Christ. The general pattern of revelation in the Bible is that when God acts he explains what he is doing beforehand, while he is doing it and immediately afterwards, and the Bible sees that this revelation points to the coming of the Lord Jesus. Calvin summarizes God's activity of revelation by quoting Hebrews 1:1–2: 'In the past God spoke to our forefathers through the prophets at many times and in various ways, but in these last days he has spoken to us by his Son, whom he appointed heir of all things, and through whom he made the universe.' Calvin comments:

> God will not speak hereafter as he did before, intermittently through some and through others; nor will he add prophecies to prophecies, or revelations to revelations. Rather, he has so fulfilled all functions of teaching in his Son that we must regard this as the final and eternal testimony from him.[12]

If Christ is the fullness of God's revelation, then the words about Christ in Scripture are the means by which God explains his Word, his Son the Lord Jesus. If, as Paul says, 'no matter how many promises God has made, they are "Yes" in Christ' (2 Cor. 1:20), then we need no further words after Christ's apostles to understand the meaning of God's action in Christ. As Jewel says of Scripture:

> There is no sentence, no clause, no word, no syllable; no letter, but it is written for thy instruction; there is not one jot, but it is sealed and signed with the blood of the Lamb. Our imaginations are idle, our thoughts are vain; there is no idleness nor no vanity in the Word of God.[13]

34

So the doctrine of the *sufficiency of Scripture* is inextricably linked to the doctrine of the *sufficiency of Christ*. In Christ God has acted and has made through him a sufficient sacrifice for the sins of the whole world. In the Bible God has spoken and provided a sufficient explanation of Christ and his sacrifice, and has thus provided the message of the gospel of Christ for the whole world. God has acted sufficiently for our salvation; God has spoken sufficiently for our salvation. We believe in the sufficient works and words of God.

Of course, this doctrine of the sufficiency of Christ and the sufficiency of Scripture should not be taken to mean that the activities of God are confined to the past. Christ died once for all, but he applies his saving work done on the cross to human lives from his seat at the Father's right hand in glory; God has spoken through prophets and apostles and through his Son, but he still speaks to us through these words spoken so long ago.

We can see then that the doctrine of the sufficiency of Scripture is tied to the sufficiency of Christ. In the words of the hymn:

> How firm a foundation, ye saints of the Lord,
> Is laid for your faith in his excellent word;
> What more can he say than to you he hath said,
> You who unto Jesus for refuge have fled?[14]

2. The argument from salvation history

The argument from salvation history is in a sense another form of the same argument. As Herman Bavinck writes:

> Christ is the fulfilment of all . . . first of all in his person and appearance, then in his words and works, in his birth and life, in his death and resurrection, in his ascension and sitting at the right hand of God. If then he has appeared, and has finished his work, the revelation of God cannot be amplified or be increased, it can only be clarified by the apostolic witness and preached to all nations. Since the revelation is complete, the time is now come in which its content is made the property of mankind . . . And this dispensation continues until the fullness of the Gentiles is come and Israel is saved.[15]

From an eschatological perspective we must say that we now see through a glass darkly (1 Cor. 13:12), and that it does not yet appear what we shall be (1 Jn. 3:2), but that all that God is doing in the present time is explained in Scripture. There are no new actions of God, no further revelations that he will make, until the Lord Jesus returns. We are living in the last days, the days of the Son and his

Spirit. There is no third age or further revelation. So Christ warns against those who pretend to further revelation. 'At that time if anyone says to you, "Look, here is the Christ!" or, "Look, there he is!" do not believe it. For false Christs and false prophets will appear and perform signs and miracles to deceive the elect – if that were possible. So be on your guard; I have told you everything ahead of time' (Mk. 13:21–23).

3. The argument from Scripture

Again and again in the pages of the Bible we find the writers asserting that their own words do not need to be complemented; they speak the words of God. Thus Jeremiah condemns the false prophets:

> This is what the LORD Almighty says:
>
> 'Do not listen to what the prophets are prophesying to you;
>   they fill you with false hopes.
> They speak visions from their own minds,
>   not from the mouth of the LORD.
> They keep saying to those who despise me,
>   "The LORD says: You will have peace."
> And to all who follow the stubbornness of their hearts
>   they say, "No harm will come to you."
> But which of them has stood in the council of the LORD
>   to see or to hear his word?
> Who has listened and heard his word?'   (Je. 23:16–18)

The people of God have to discern what is the true revelation of God, who is the true prophet and who are the false prophets. If they try and add together all the words of all the prophets they hear, without discernment, they will be very confused about what God is saying and probably conclude that God is incapable of revealing his will to his people.

The doctrine of the sufficiency of Scripture is also the subject of Jesus' teaching in Mark 7. The issue under debate is whether Jesus' Scripture (that is, the Old Testament) is a sufficient guide for the people of God or whether its teaching needs to be supplemented by many 'other traditions' or 'traditions of the elders' represented by the Pharisees or teachers of the law.

Jesus tackles the issue by asserting the freedom and independence of the Word of God over and against the verbal traditions of the religious leaders of his day. But he does not regard their alternative form of tradition as neutral. It is in fact opposed to the Word of God. So he says, 'You have let go of the commands of God and are holding on to the traditions of men' (Mk. 7:8), and later, 'Thus you nullify the word of God by your tradition that you have handed down. And you do many things like that' (Mk. 7:13). He summarizes his condemnation of their teaching with the words of Isaiah: 'These people honour me with their lips, but their hearts are far from me. They worship me in vain; their teachings are but rules taught by men' (Mk. 7:6–7).

In summary, then, Jesus' accusation against those who hold a dual deposit of God's teaching is that they let go the commands of God, set aside the commands of God and nullify the word of God. Jesus teaches the sufficiency of his Scripture. In general the New Testament writers identify their apostolic teaching about Jesus as the gospel, and to move from their gospel is to move away from Christ. 'But even if we or an angel from heaven should preach a gospel other than the one we preached to you, let him be eternally condemned!' (Gal. 1:8). 'For if someone comes to you and preaches a Jesus other than the Jesus we preached, or if you receive a different spirit from the one you received, or a different gospel from the one you accepted, you put up with it easily enough' (2 Cor. 11:4).

In the light of this evidence it is instructive to see how the Bible writers analyse the issue of the sufficiency of Scripture. Some who teach the insufficiency of Scripture argue that it needs to be complemented by other revelations from God. The Bible makes it clear that complementary ideas come from the minds of humans, not God, and their effect is to undermine or nullify the Word of God.

Of course, the verse which is beloved of those who want to teach the doctrine of supplementary revelation, of God's continuous guidance of the church into more and more truth beyond that found in Scripture, is John 16:13: 'But when he, the Spirit of truth, comes, he will guide you into all truth.' But it is very important to read this verse in context. The speaker is the Lord Jesus, and the subject is the teaching that he has given to the disciples. He is explaining that he has not been able to teach them everything, but that they will be led into all truth after the resurrection by the coming of the Spirit of God. This promise is fulfilled in the work of the apostles and prophets of the early church in making clear what God has done through Christ. We understand the rest of Jesus' teaching in John 14 – 16 as having particular application to its original audience, so we should not make an exception for these particular words.

We read in the Homily that some argue

> . . . that there are diverse necessary points not expressed in Holy Scripture, which were left to the revelation of the Holy Ghost . . . To this we may easily answer by the plain words of Christ, teaching us that the proper office of the Holy Ghost is, not to institute and bring in new ordinances, contrary to

his doctrine before taught, but to expound and declare those things which he had before taught, so that they might be well and truly understood.[16]

The doctrine of the sufficiency of Scripture was clearly a major issue at the Reformation, where the motto *sola Scriptura* was an attempt to refute the authority of the traditions appealed to by the church of Rome. As Berkouwer points out, *sola Scriptura* was also closely tied to *sola fide* (faith alone), *sola gratia* (grace alone), and *solo Christo* (Christ alone).[17]

The doctrine of the sufficiency of Scripture is a way of safeguarding the truth about Christ and the truth about the gospel.

Another way of asserting the sufficiency of Scripture is to look back over the history of the church during the last 2,000 years and ask: what new doctrines have been asserted over that period? Some such doctrines have attempted to explain the meaning of Scripture (for example, the doctrine of the Trinity and the Christological statements of the early church). But another class of doctrine has included those which have been asserted independently of Scripture. The list includes doctrines which must be regarded as having hindered Christian truth and maturity and not furthered it, such as the doctrine of the mass, the infallibility of the pope, the assumption of Mary, and many denominational statements about their particular pattern of church life and order which have taken on an authority equivalent to, or superior to, that of Scripture. The doctrines which are additional to God's Word in Scripture are clearly unhelpful. This would lead the casual observer to think that the methodology of adding revelation to Scripture is an unwise one.

It is an unhappy characteristic of those who hold to the equal authority of their denominational traditions and Scripture that in practice they demand greater loyalty to those traditions than they do to Scripture. So some Anglicans are dogmatic about the threefold order of ministry and a particular doctrine of the eucharist, while maintaining scepticism about the incarnation or atonement. Some Baptists value baptism by immersion more highly than the Trinity, and some Presbyterians value a system of church government more highly than the resurrection of Christ.

There is much that is useful in Alister McGrath's and David Wenham's chapter on biblical authority in *Evangelical Anglicans: Their Role and Influence in the Church Today*, not least in their attempt to show that the evangelical commitment to the authority of Scripture represents historic, mainline Christianity. But a few sentences seem to me to represent a significant retreat from the traditional doctrine of the sufficiency of Scripture. They write that 'Scripture defines the centre of gravity of evangelicalism, not the limits of its reading or knowledge'.[18] Of course our reading and knowledge are wider than Scripture, but our certain knowledge of salvation is found and substantiated only by God in Scripture. They continue: 'Scripture is . . . the central legitimating resource of Christian faith and theology, the clearest window through which the face of Christ may be seen.'[19] I think the words 'central', 'resource' and 'clearest' somewhat weak. For, under God, Scripture is the *only* authoritative interpretation of Christ that we have, not just a central resource or the clearest window.

Scripture sufficient and effective

What then are the implications of the doctrine of the sufficiency of Scripture and the belief that Scripture will effect the purposes for which it was written by God?

First, the Bible contains its own message of the gospel, and thus the best form of evangelism is the preaching and teaching of the Bible: 'But these are written that you may believe that Jesus is the Christ, the Son of God, and that by believing you may have life in his name' (Jn. 20:31).

Secondly, the result of preaching and teaching the Bible will be the edification of God's people and their equipment for every good work: 'All Scripture is God-breathed and is useful for teaching, rebuking, correcting and training in righteousness, so that the man of God may be thoroughly equipped for every good work' (2 Tim. 3:16–17). Congregations will be not only brought to maturity in faith but also equipped for effective Christian ministry through the teaching and preaching of the Bible.

Thirdly, because God through the Bible trains us for Christian ministry, the Bible itself ought to be the main teaching tool of our theological colleges which aim to equip people for effective Christian ministry, and ought to set the agenda for our learning.

Finally, the main aim of training ought to be to help us use the Bible well in the church and in the world, in gospel ministry.

A Festschrift like this provides a good opportunity to study a great theme such as that of preaching, and also to ask whether the theory works in practice. It is a way of testing the practical usefulness of a profound theology. It gives us the excuse to ask: in what ways has the doctrine of the sufficiency of Scripture informed the preaching of Dick Lucas? In what ways is he an exemplar of the doctrine which has been asserted in these pages? I think we can see the following expressions of the doctrine in his preaching ministry.

First, he has demonstrated a profound commitment to the

sufficiency of Scripture in basing all his public ministry on the exposition of Scripture, in preaching through sections, books and chapters of the Bible, and in finding in this a more than adequate way of doing evangelism and promoting the edification of individuals and of the church of God.

Secondly, his preaching has not been merely a historical explanation of the sufficient Scripture, but has always been strong on application, or what he would call the implications of the text. That is, the sufficient Scripture has been taught not as merely historical revelation but as the present Word of God to his people. Dick Lucas has been creative and imaginative, and one might almost say prophetic, in the way in which he has challenged the assumptions of our society and of our Christian traditions directly from the Word of God. It is often assumed that expository preaching is mainly concerned with the explanation of the text. In fact, Dick Lucas, in his preaching, spends at least half and sometimes two thirds of his time drawing out the implications of the text for the people who are listening.

Thirdly, the great theme of his preaching has been that the Bible is sufficient not only to start people off in Christian living but also to bring them to maturity. A common accusation made against evangelicals is that they can teach enough of the gospel to enable people to begin as Christians, but that real maturity of faith needs to be found beyond their simple doctrines and beyond the pages of the Bible. Dick Lucas has shown again and again that God has provided everything we need for Christian living and for full maturity in Christ, and that there is sufficient teaching about this maturity in the Bible.

Fourthly, in an age when there are disputes about an appropriate pattern of ministry in our contemporary society, Dick Lucas has shown again and again that God has provided a sufficient pattern of ministry in the Scriptures, and has challenged us to review our priorities and practices in ministry by what God has taught us in the Bible. In the words of John Newton, another distinguished City of London rector with a nautical background: 'Real communion with the Lord in his appointed means of grace is likewise an important branch of . . . blessedness. The Scriptures were instituted for this end, and are sufficient, by virtue of his power and Spirit, to answer it.'[20]

Throughout his ministry, Dick Lucas has remained an unlikely revolutionary, an unexpected radical. He always speaks with a radical power and effectiveness because of his commitment to the doctrine of the sufficiency of Scripture, because he is determined to test everything by Scripture, and because he puts his belief in the sufficiency and effectiveness of Scripture into practice in his preaching and teaching ministry. In this he represents the best tradition of the people of God, that of loyalty to Scripture alone as God's Word written:

Let us diligently search for the well of life in the books of the New and Old Testament, and not run to the stinking puddles of men's traditions, devised by man's imagination, for our justification and salvation. For in holy Scripture is fully contained what we ought to do and what to eschew, what to believe, what to love, and what to look for at God's hands at length. In those books we shall find the Father, from whom, the Son, by whom, and the Holy Ghost, in whom, all things have their being and keeping up; and these three Persons to be but one God and one substance. In these books we may learn to know ourselves, how vile and miserable we be; and also to know God, how good he is of himself, and how he maketh us and all creatures partakers of his goodness. We may learn also in these books to know God's will and pleasure, as much as for this present time is convenient for us to know. And, as the great clerk and godly preacher St. John Chrysostom saith, 'whatsoever is required to salvation of man is fully contained in the Scripture of God. He that is ignorant may there learn and have knowledge. He that is hard hearted and an obstinate sinner shall there find everlasting torments prepared of God's justice, to make him afraid, and to mollify (or soften) him. He that is oppressed with misery in this world shall there find relief in the promises of everlasting life, to his great consolation and comfort. He that is wounded by the devil unto death shall find the medicine, whereby he may be restored again unto health.' 'If it shall require to teach any truth or reprove false doctrines, to rebuke any vice, to commend any virtue, to give good counsel, to comfort, or to exhort, or to do any other thing requisite for our salvation; all those things,' saith St. Chrysostom, 'we may learn plentifully of the Scriptures.'[21]

Notes

1. Ordinal: The Form of Ordaining or Consecrating of an Archbishop or Bishop (1662).

2. Thomas K. Carroll, *Preaching the Word* (Wilmington: Michael Glazier, 1984), pp. 63, 197, 206.

3. *The Decades of Henry Bullinger*, 1 (Cambridge: Cambridge University Press, 1849), p. 61 (my emphasis). See also Noel Weeks, *The Sufficiency of Scripture* (Edinburgh: Banner of Truth, 1988).

4. John Calvin, *Institutes of the Christian Religion*, Library of Christian Classics (ET Philadelphia: Westminster, 1960), IV.i.5, p. 1018.

5. *Ibid.*, IV.iii.1, p. 1054.

6. *Idem, Sermons on Timothy and Titus* (1579; ET Edinburgh: Banner of Truth, 1983), p. 945.

7. *Ibid.*, p. 947.

8. *Ibid.*, p. 1199.

9. *Dogmatic Constitution on Divine Revelation*, in Austin Flannery (ed.), *Vatican Council II: The Conciliar and Post-Conciliar Documents* (Dublin: Dominican Publications, 1975), p. 755.

10. *Ibid.*

11. John Jewel, 'Of the Holy Scriptures', in *The Writings of John Jewel* (London: Religious Tract Society, n.d.), pp. 58–62.

12. Calvin, *Institutes* IV.viii.7, pp. 1154–1155.

13. Jewel, *op. cit.*, p. 58.

14. Richard Keen, 'How Firm a Foundation' (*c.* 1787).

15. Herman Bavinck, *Our Reasonable Faith* (Grand Rapids: Baker, 1976), p. 94.

16. The Second Part of the Sermon for Whitsunday, 'An Homily Concerning the Coming Down of the Holy Ghost and the Manifold Gifts of the Same': *Second Book of Homilies* (1571), in *Certain Sermons or Homilies Appointed to be Read in Churches* (London: SPCK, 1864), p. 497. I am indebted to Allan Chapple for this reference.

17. G. C. Berkouwer, *Holy Scripture* (Grand Rapids: Eerdmans, 1975), p. 302.

18. In R. T. France and A. E. McGrath (eds.), *Evangelical Anglicans: Their Role and Influence in the Church Today* (London: SPCK, 1993), p. 27.

19. *Ibid.*

20. John Newton, *Collected Letters*, ed. H. Backhouse (London: Hodder and Stoughton, 1989), p. 127. I am indebted to Allan Chapple for this reference.

21. 'The First Part of the Exhortation to the Reading of Holy Scripture', *(First) Book of Homilies* (1547), in *op. cit.*, pp. 2–3.

3

The preacher and the living Word

Preaching and the Holy Spirit

John Woodhouse

For you have been born again, not of perishable seed, but of imperishable, through the living and enduring word of God . . . And this is the word that was preached to you. (1 Pet. 1:23, 25)

We also have had the gospel preached to us . . . the word of God is living and active . . . (Heb. 4:2, 12)

The purpose of this essay is to explore the 'living' character of the preached Word of God. What is meant by this expression? What makes preaching 'alive' in this sense? Can the 'life' be taken out of preaching? How?

It would be a mistake to answer these questions superficially. All of us have heard (and many of us have engaged in) preaching which is *dull*. We who preach might want to acknowledge with shame (and our hearers might well confirm our confession) that much modern preaching is *deadly* dull. And we long to hear preaching that is *alive*! By this we mean preaching that is interesting, gripping, relevant and with at least a touch of excitement.

The New Testament writers, however, did not have that in mind when they referred to the preached Word as 'living'. It is not the rhetorical skills of the preacher that make the Word of God 'living' (see 1 Cor. 2:1–5). The Word of God is 'living' because it is the living God who speaks it (see 1 Thes. 2:13).

A failure to understand this reality will inevitably lead (and has inevitably led?) to a decline in preaching, both in its quality and in its place in the life of the churches. At stake here is the very nature of the Christian religion and the character of the Christian experience of God. Many, who have failed to understand that it is *God* who is speaking when the Word *of God* is heard, have (understandably) become dissatisfied with a religion in which the Bible is studied merely as a source of information, and have turned to seek God himself in experiences other than the hearing of his Word. Christian experience is then distorted into sacramentalism, or some form of mysticism, or both.

Evangelical Christianity (which claims to be no less than biblical Christianity, and therefore authentic Christianity) understands that the Word of God is no mere 'dead letter', but is 'living', for it is the Word of the living God. God cannot be separated from his Word. It would then cease to be *his* Word, at least in this biblical sense. To hear the Word *of God* is to encounter God as fully and as really as is possible for a human being. But is this what is happening in our churches? Is this what is happening through our preaching? If not, why not?

In this essay I want to suggest that a renewed appreciation (and practice) of preaching the 'living' Word of God depends on a proper understanding of the relationship between the Word of God and the Spirit of God.[1]

The call for 'balance'

The contemporary failure to understand the intimate relationship between the Word and the Spirit of God is particularly evident in the modern controversy among 'evangelicals' and 'charismatics'. Each side of this deeply felt debate seems to have an emphasis on an important theological reality which it believes the other is neglecting. The evangelical emphasis (by definition) is on the Word of God, in the form of the Scriptures. The charismatic emphasis is on the Spirit of God. The charismatic caricature of the evangelical is that he or she has intellectualized the faith into understanding propositions. The corresponding evangelical estimate of the charismatic is that he or she is living in a world of make-believe, making too much of relatively unimportant experiences.

A common response to this confusion is to call for 'balance'. The reasoning goes like this. There are some evangelicals who over-emphasize the Word and underemphasize the Spirit. Theirs is a dull, unemotional Christianity, with no vitality, doctrinally pure but dead, squeaky clean from error but sterile. Then there are those who overemphasize the Spirit and undervalue the Word. The result? Froth and bubble. Emotionalism and chaos: certainly not dull, but at times indistinguishable from pagan orgies. What we need is to redress the *balance*. Both 'imbalances' need to be corrected. Those who love the Word must be brought to life by the Spirit, while those who enjoy the Spirit must be disciplined by the Word. The truth lies, on this view, in *balancing* the opposite extremes, in the middle ground of truth.

I have based this description on a recent evangelical publication on the issue. But surely this analysis cannot be right.

Is there not a problem with calling the Word *of God* dead, sterile and lacking in vitality? *We* may be dull and dead. But it cannot be right to attribute our dullness and death (and I agree that there is plenty of it around) to an overemphasis on the Word that the living God speaks to his people. No less serious is the suggestion that the work of the Spirit of God is froth and bubble. Can it be right to attribute chaotic emotionalism, barely distinguishable from pagan orgies (and there is plenty of that around too), to the Holy Spirit of God?

What is needed is not a *balance* between death and pagan orgies. This is a case where the truth of the matter is not found along the path of 'balance'. For the balance, if it were ever attained, would probably be an error more subtle than either of those already described. It will appear both alive and doctrinally correct, but may have neither the Word of God nor the Spirit of God.

The problem is that 'balance' is not a very helpful key for sorting out truth. I cannot think of any occasion when the New Testament writers employ this notion in dealing with aberrations of authentic Christianity. Jesus was not crucified for too much balance. From the perspective of his accusers he was a dangerous extremist. Of all the perfections attributed to him in the New Testament, 'balance' is conspicuously absent. Christian truth is always likely to appear extreme to those who do not agree with it.

I assert this, not because I want to promote 'imbalance' in the Christian life, or because I want to suggest that there is no such thing as 'imbalance', or because I want to undermine efforts at mutual understanding; but because I believe that the idea of 'balance' is not as useful as we sometimes think. And that is not surprising if, as I am suggesting, it is not a biblical way of thinking. The problem is that any belief looks 'balanced' to the person who holds it. What is 'balanced' is an entirely subjective judgment. Of course Jesus appears 'balanced', if you agree with him. But to his opponents he is imbalanced. That is, there are always equal and opposite deviations from one's belief. But the position midway between two errors is not always the truth. More often it is a third error, possibly more dangerous than the other two.

In the particular case of the Word of God and the Spirit of God, simply to call for 'balance' is to miss the point. The important, not to say urgent, task is to examine the Scriptures to understand the *relationship* between the Word of God and the Spirit of God. Perhaps both sides of the debate are in error. Neither would admit, of course, to neglecting either the Word or the Spirit, but might not the problem arise from a failure to understand the *relationship* between the two?

In other words, the problem seems to have a dimension that will not be solved by telling evangelicals to put more emphasis on the Spirit, and charismatics to put more emphasis on the Word. That would not bring the two sides closer together, in my opinion. There are differences which are more than the *degree of emphasis* on either the Spirit or the Word.

The Spirit and the Word: a neglected theme

The fact that the Spirit of God and the Word of God are intimately related in the Bible has been widely recognized, and has had an important place in theological understanding. Certainly it was important for Luther[2] and Calvin[3] in the Reformation period. But, as such, it is not a distinctively Protestant theme in theology; the link between the two is too obvious in Scripture for that.[4]

It seems fair to say, however, that evangelicals have at times neglected the relationship between God's Word and God's Spirit. This is understandable. The controversies about the doctrine of the Word of God in which evangelicals have found themselves engaged during this century have required careful attention to the fundamental issues of the Scriptures' authority, inspiration and truth. This has meant that the work of the Holy Spirit has received attention in connection with the inspiration of Scripture and the 'inner witness' of the Spirit to the Scriptures' authority.[5] But it might be argued that even here the Spirit's work has not received the specifically biblical attention that has rightly been given to questions of authority and truth. One conclusion in this essay will be that an even more intimate and extensive relationship should be recognized between the Spirit and the Word than is found in most contemporary evangelical writing about either the Word or the Spirit of God. A biblical doctrine of the Word of God must necessarily be integrated with the doctrine of the Spirit of God, and, conversely, a biblical understanding of the Spirit of God is inseparable from the concept of God's Word. The Word is the Spirit's implement, and the Spirit is the breath by which God speaks.

The argument will take the following course. It will first be established that the Word of God is fundamental to and formative of all God's dealings with his world and his people. The relationship between the Word of God and the Spirit of God will then be explored, and we will see that the Word of God is 'living' precisely because of the Spirit's presence and work.

God and his Word

There can be no argument that in the Bible God's *Word* is fundamentally important. Wherever we turn in the Bible we find this extraordinary phenomenon: the *Word* of God.

Creation and the Word of God

Perhaps we are too familiar with Genesis 1 to notice that the Bible's description of creation is striking because of this very point: God created the world by *speaking*. There were many other ways in which the ancient world thought of the gods bringing the cosmos into being. Some saw it as an emanation from the thought of the deity; others saw it as an outcome of the activity of the deity, often in battle with opponents. The Bible, however, says that God spoke: 'God said, "Let there be light," and there was light' (Gn. 1:3). At the very moment of the world's inception, we see the kind of relationship that God will have with his creation. As he brings the world into being, God's 'point of contact' with his creation is his *Word*. God is not found in creation itself. Neither is God so removed from creation that there is no link. His *Word* is the link, the point of contact. Throughout the Scriptures of the Old and New Testaments, in a variety of ways, this concept is found: God speaks, and his Word relates him to his creation, by conveying and enacting his will towards his creation.

> By the word of the LORD were the heavens made,
>   their starry host by the breath of his mouth . . .
> For he spoke, and it came to be;
>   he commanded and it stood firm.   (Ps. 33:6, 9)

> But at your rebuke the waters fled . . . (Ps. 104:7)

> Your word, O LORD, is eternal;
>   it stands firm in the heavens.
> Your faithfulness continues through all generations;
>   you established the earth, and it endures.   (Ps. 119:89–90)

... sustaining all things by his powerful word. (Heb. 1:3)

... long ago by God's word the heavens existed and the earth was formed out of water and by water. (2 Pet. 3:5)

A moment's reflection will show that this is a very profound truth. At the very point at which God is least like us – as creator distinct from his creatures, as the upholder in contrast to the upheld – it is the Word of God that bridges the gap. He brings into being by speaking, he shapes and forms by speaking, he upholds it all by speaking. This is no impersonal 'force', or the transcendent 'other', or one who is found by inner contemplation. It is the speaking of God which is fundamental in his relationship to his creation.

Israel and the Word of God

It is no coincidence, then, that the history of Israel was set in motion by God speaking. This time, however, there were differences. God spoke, not to his cosmic creation, but to one man, Abram. And his Word was not so much a command ('Let there be light') – although a command was involved ('Leave your country . . . and go to the land I will show you') – as a promise ('I will make you into a great nation . . . and all peoples on earth will be blessed through you'; Gn. 12:1, 3). And the course of biblical history is the tracing out of the fulfilment of that promise. God has spoken, and those to whom he spoke were now to live under his Word. What God said was to shape their lives and destinies.

It was in accordance with his promise that God brought the Israelites to Mount Sinai in the days of Moses, where they were constituted, as it were, God's people. And what happened at Mount Sinai provided the basis for Israel's understanding of the principle we have already seen, and for how it was to work out in their experience. This is explained with remarkable clarity by Moses in Deuteronomy 4.

You came near and stood at the foot of the mountain while it blazed with fire to the very heavens, with black clouds and deep darkness. Then the LORD spoke to you out of the fire. You heard the sound of words but saw no form; there was only a voice. He declared to you his covenant, the Ten Commandments, which he commanded you to follow and then wrote them on two stone tablets. And the LORD directed me at that time to teach you the decrees and laws you are to follow in the land that you are crossing the Jordan to possess.

You saw no form of any kind the day the LORD spoke to

you at Horeb out of the fire. Therefore watch yourselves very carefully, so that you do not become corrupt and make for yourselves an idol, an image of any shape, whether formed like a man' or a woman, or like any animal on earth or any bird that flies in the air, or like any creature that moves along the ground or any fish in the waters below. (Dt. 4:11–18)

God had *spoken*, and the only valid response was to hear and heed. This is the problem with idolatry, in its ancient and modern forms. It is not just that God is invisible and so cannot be represented visibly. The basic problem with idolatry is that God has *spoken*. Making an idol is not only stupid (as the prophets delight in saying); it is *corrupt*, because it disregards the manner of God's dealing with us.

The nature of true relationship with God and authentic experience of God is determined by the nature of God's revelation. If God has approached us by speaking, then to know God is to hear and heed his Word.

The Word of God in the New Testament

With the coming of Jesus Christ, the content of God's Word to humankind was radically sharpened and clarified, and the boundaries of those addressed by God's Word exploded from Israel to all the nations on earth. But it did not cease to be a *Word*. It is in the gospel Word that the righteousness of God is revealed (Rom. 1:17). Through the pages of the New Testament it is clear that the Word of God, the word of the gospel, the word of the cross, is on centre stage.

What is the essence of the apostolic ministry in the New Testament?

Christ did not send me to baptise, but to *preach the gospel* – not with words of human wisdom, lest the cross of Christ be emptied of its power.

For *the message of the cross* is foolishness to those who are perishing, but to us who are being saved it is the power of God. (1 Cor. 1:17–18)

Therefore, since through God's mercy we have this ministry, we do not lose heart. Rather, we have renounced secret and shameful ways; we do not use deception, nor do we distort *the word of God*. On the contrary, by setting forth the truth plainly we commend ourselves to every man's conscience in the sight of God. (2 Cor. 4:1–2)

What activity brings most joy to the heart of the apostle?

Now I want you to know, brothers, that what has happened to me has really served to advance the gospel . . . Because of my chains, most of the brothers in the Lord have been encouraged to speak *the word of God* more courageously and fearlessly . . . The important thing is that in every way, whether from false motives or true, *Christ is preached*. And because of this I rejoice. (Phil. 1:12, 14, 18)

How is God at work in the life of believers?

For you have been born again, not of perishable seed, but of imperishable, through the living and enduring *word of God*. For,

> All men are like grass,
>   and all their glory is like the flowers of the field;
> the grass withers and the flowers fall,
>   but the word of the Lord stands for ever.

And this is *the word that was preached to you*. (1 Pet. 1:23–25)

And we also thank God continually because, when you received *the word of God*, which you heard from us, you accepted it not as the word of men, but as it actually is, *the word of God*, which is at work in you who believe. (1 Thes. 2:13)

For *the word of God* is living and active. Sharper than any double-edged sword, it penetrates even to dividing soul and spirit, joints and marrow; it judges the thoughts and attitudes of the heart. (Heb. 4:12)

The Word of God and human faith

That God approaches us by speaking determines the kind of relationship we have with him, the kind of experience we have of him. What is it like to be in a right relationship with God who has spoken? To be more specific: 'if God's Word turns out to be a *promise*, how then should we relate to him? Will it not be by *believing* the promise? So it is that in both Old and New Testaments, God's Word and human faith in God constitute true religion.

This is the meaning of the famous statement in Genesis 15:6, quoted by Paul in Romans 4 and Galatians 3. After Abraham had expressed his difficulty in believing God's word of promise (verses 2–3), God forcefully reiterated the promise (verses 4–5). Then we read: 'Abram believed the LORD, and he credited it to him as righteousness' (verse

6). At a turning point in the history of the world, God had spoken his Word of promise to a man. And that man believed God. In God's estimation, *that* was righteousness: man and God rightly related.[6]

What was the cause of Abraham's faith in God? It was not a virtue in Abraham for which he was rewarded with a promise. Abraham's faith was created by God. It was the *Word* of God's promise which brought Abraham to believe God. His natural response was to find the promise unbelievable. That is how Genesis 15 begins: with Abraham's doubting, unbelieving complaint. The change from doubt and unbelief in verses 2–3 to faith in verse 6 is brought about by God speaking his promise to Abraham again (verses 3–5).

Paul's letter to the Romans presents the same phenomenon: God's Word bringing about human faith in God. The letter begins:

> Paul, a servant of Christ Jesus, called to be an apostle and set apart for the gospel of God – the gospel . . . regarding his Son . . . Through him and for his name's sake, we received grace and apostleship to call people from among all the Gentiles to the obedience that comes from faith. (Rom. 1: 1–3, 5)

What is the goal of Paul's apostleship? The obedience that comes from faith among all nations. What is the means? The gospel of God: the gospel about Jesus Christ.

The doxology with which the letter concludes strikes the same note, namely that by the gospel word God will bring the nations to the obedience of faith:

> Now to him who is able to establish you by my gospel and the proclamation of Jesus Christ, according to the revelation of the mystery hidden for long ages past, but now revealed and made known through the prophetic writings by the command of the eternal God, so that all nations might believe and obey him – to the only wise God be glory for ever through Jesus Christ! Amen. (Rom. 16:25–27)

The famous thematic statement of Romans has the same focus:

> I am not ashamed of the gospel, because it is the power of God for the salvation of everyone who believes: first for the Jew, then for the Gentile. For in the gospel a righteousness from God is revealed, a righteousness that is by faith from first to last, just as it is written: 'The righteous will live by faith.' (Rom. 1:16–17)

Just as with Abraham, faith here is not a sort of 'instrument', a means to some other end. The goal of the gospel in verse 16 is (literally) 'for salvation'; in verse 17 the goal is 'for faith'. To risk labouring the point, in Romans it seems that Paul asserts that the gospel word, and faith in God brought about by the gospel word, are what Christianity is all about.

What does this tell us? Since God has spoken, right relationship with God consists in this: his Word, and our faith in him, brought about by his Word. Take away his Word, and you have nothing. You may have superstition that pretends to be faith. You may have traditions that pretend to be Christianity. You may have religious feelings. You may have wise counselling. You may have a diary filled with good works, but without the Word of God there will be no true faith in God, no right relationship with God, no authentic Christianity.

We might crystallize the point of all this in a simple proposition: *Where the Word of God brings about faith in God, there is biblical Christianity. Where the Word of God is lacking, there is no Christianity.*

The Spirit of God

The question arises from what has been said so far: what then is the place of *experience* in the Christian life? What transforms the academic study of *words* into the 'living and active' Word of God? These days many would suggest that our emphasis on the Word so far seems to be at the expense of the Spirit. Is this not precisely the typical evangelical problem? The proposition should read (it might be suggested): *Where the Word of God brings about faith in God* AND *an openness to the experience of the Spirit of God, then you have something closer to biblical Christianity.*

Such a response raises the question sharply: what *is* the work of the Spirit in the Christian life? What experiences are the experience of the Spirit of God? And how do these things relate to the Word of God? For the contemporary danger is that all manner of experiences are being claimed to be experiences of the Holy Spirit. But how is the claim to be tested?

Experience and the Word of God

It is important to notice that much of this kind of thinking makes a mistake from the very beginning. It draws a false dichotomy between 'experience' and the Word of God. For the fundamental Christian experience is the *experience of the Word of God.*

In New Testament times the Christians were often described with reference to the *experience* of the Word of God that distinguished them. There are several expressions like this in the New Testament. One of them is 'the called ones' or 'those who are called'. The expression can be used simply and without any further explanation. For the Christians, the experience of having been *called* was so distinctive and all-embracing that it identified them. The reference is, of course, to being called by God through the gospel word. What an experience that is: to have heard the gospel, and to have realized that one was being addressed not by man, but by God himself!

> Jude, a servant of Jesus Christ and a brother of James,
> *To those who have been called*, who are loved by God the
> Father and kept by Jesus Christ. (Jude 1)

> We preach Christ crucified: a stumbling-block to Jews and
> foolishness to Gentiles, but to *those whom God has called*, both
> Jews and Greeks, Christ the power of God and the wisdom of
> God. (1 Cor. 1:23–24)

This was such a distinctive experience that one way of referring to God was in these terms:

> *The one who calls you* is faithful and he will do it. (1 Thes.
> 5:24)

> I am astonished that you are so quickly deserting *the one who
> called you* . . . (Gal. 1:6)

> But you are a chosen people, a royal priesthood, a holy
> nation, a people belonging to God, that you may declare the
> praises of *him who called you* out of darkness into his
> wonderful light. (1 Pet. 2:9)

This is an experience known to every Christian person. The pity is that we have sometimes come to regard it lightly. It seems that the New Testament writers were anxious to remind believers that not only have we been *called by God*, but he continues to *call* us into his kingdom and glory by the gospel.[7]

There is another very wonderful, and apparently favourite, expression for Christians in the New Testament that refers to them by a characteristic experience. Christians are called 'believers'. They are people who have *this* experience: *faith in God*. It is of course bound up with the experience of being called. Christians know themselves to have been addressed by God, and what God has said to them in the gospel has brought them to the experience of faith in God, an experience that cannot be surpassed. So the proposition that 'where there is the Word

53

of God and faith in God because of that Word, there is the totality of Christianity' is not anti-experiential. On the contrary, it focuses on the central definitive and continuing experience of the Christian life.

But what about the Spirit?

What then is to be made of the objection that this narrow emphasis on the Word is at the expense of the Spirit? It is argued that the arid tedium of much evangelical Christianity is seen right here: the emphasis on the Word has produced a religion of the mind only. Our preachers are more like lecturers than Spirit-anointed prophets, and our Bible studies are more like literary seminars than encounters with the living God. 'You may have the *Word*, but you cannot tell me that that is all there is to Christianity.' 'Without the Spirit the Word is sterile.'

When this inadequacy is felt (as it is being felt by many today), Christian lives and ministries begin to take on a new shape. The Christian life begins to develop in a new way. There is, of course, a *Word* dimension, but people begin to seek the missing *Spirit* dimension. These may not be completely unrelated, but they are nevertheless viewed as distinct and different. The minister still studies his Bible and preaches it, but he is also 'led by the Spirit', which is understood to be something distinct. Christians still read their Bibles and listen to sermons. But another level of experience is sought – not necessarily unrelated to the first, but distinct and different – an experience of the Spirit. Christian meetings – church – can be structured round these two supposedly distinct dimensions of Christian experience. On the one hand there is the reading of the Bible with the sermon, and on the other there can be a time when the Spirit of God is expected to come and do something more. It has been described to me like this: 'Of course God meets us in his Word. But that is not the only way in which he deals with us. There is another dimension, a more *direct* working of God – almost a more tangible working, by his Spirit.' This line of thinking, and the implications it has for Christian life and ministry, are mistaken in a most serious way.

It is certainly possible to have an emphasis on words (even the words of the Bible) which is inadequate. There can be truth in the objection I am describing. I can study the historical and cultural background of the letters to the seven churches; I can explain the literary structure of the letter to the Romans; I can weave jokes and illustrations round a passage from the gospels; I can talk about the meanings of Greek and Hebrew words. And all this can have to do with the Bible. But I have not necessarily encountered, or conveyed, the Word of God. All those things can aid understanding the Word of God, but they are not themselves the Word of God. One can receive the word of the Bible without receiving it as it really is, the Word of God (*cf.* 1 Thes. 2:13).

54

Likewise we can teach the word of the Bible without teaching it as it really is, the Word of God. And we can study the word of the Bible without studying it as it really is, the Word of God. Much scholarly study of the Bible falls into precisely this category. The form, the history, the language of the Bible can be studied and taught, without receiving the Bible's message as it actually is, the Word that God is speaking.

There have been times when we evangelicals have fallen into the error of studying the words of the Bible *for their own sake*. The words must not be separated from the Speaker and given autonomy. The words of the Bible matter, but precisely because they are the words *of God*. A 'Christianity' that has become interested in the words, but not in the Speaker of the words, is certainly not biblical Christianity. But the problem is that the words are not being received as they really are, the words *of God*. We do not need to go looking for something to balance this emphasis on God's Word. We do not need to try to meet God in some other way, as though we do not fully or adequately meet him as he speaks his Word to us. We need to give proper, humble, receptive attention to the living God who addresses his Word to us.

What about the Spirit? Is not my earlier description of Christianity still clearly and hopelessly inadequate, and obviously so, because I have still left the Spirit out of account? While I have not yet explained the Spirit's role explicitly, all that has been said so far is about the work of the Spirit. Where there is the Word of God there is always the Spirit of God. We need to explore the relationship between God's Spirit and God's Word in the Bible.

Breath and speech

One problem for us in understanding this connection is that English lacks a word which has the range of meaning of the Hebrew *rûah* and the Greek *pneuma*. Both these words can mean 'wind' and 'breath' as well as 'spirit'. In many biblical texts the expression 'the Spirit of God' could be well translated 'the breath of God'. We will see, then, that in biblical thought the Spirit of God is as closely connected to the Word of God as breath is connected to speech.

In creation. The connection is suggested in the very first words of Genesis:

> In the beginning God created the heavens and the earth. The earth was without form and void, and darkness was upon the face of the deep; and the Spirit [breath; Hebrew *rûah*] of God was moving over the face of the waters.
>
> And God said, 'Let there be light'; and there was light. (Gn. 1:1–3, RSV)

The connection between verses 2 and 3 is much debated among scholars, but the semantic association between *rûaḥ* (verse 2) and speech (verse 3) is often overlooked. When the psalmist reflects on God's wonderful work of creation in Psalm 33, he makes exactly the same connection:

> By the word of the LORD were the heavens made,
>> their starry host by the breath [Hebrew *rûaḥ*] of his mouth.
>>> (Ps. 33:6)

Other Old Testament examples. In Isaiah 34:16 we find a poetic parallelism between 'the [speaking] mouth of the LORD' and 'his Spirit':

> For the mouth of the LORD has commanded,
>> and his Spirit [breath; Hebrew *rûaḥ*] has gathered them (RSV).

'Spirit' here (in English versions) refers to the breath of God's command (as in Ps. 33:6).

More clearly still, consider Isaiah 59:21:

> 'And as for me, this is my covenant with them,' says the LORD. 'My Spirit [breath; Hebrew *rûaḥ*] who is on you, and my word that I have put in your mouth will not depart from your mouth, or from the mouths of your children, or from the mouths of their descendants from this time on and for ever,' says the LORD.

Here it is not too much to say that 'my Spirit who is on you' and 'my words that I have put in your mouth' amount to the same thing. They are used interchangeably. Both expressions are the subject of 'will not depart from your mouth'.

The connection is maintained in the important text of Isaiah 61:1:

> The Spirit [breath; Hebrew *rûaḥ*] of the Sovereign LORD is
>> upon me,
>> because the LORD has anointed me
> to preach good news to the poor . . .

Notice the 'because'. Jesus quotes this prophecy in Luke 4:18, where 'Spirit' translates Greek *pneuma*, 'breath'. This is the same as saying: 'He has anointed me to proclaim the gospel; *therefore* the Spirit of the Lord is upon me.' The logic is that where the Word of God is, there the Spirit (or breath) of God is also. For one's word cannot be separated from one's breath.

The New Testament. The connection between Spirit and Word flows on into the New Testament. Jesus said:

> The one whom God has sent speaks the *words* of God, for he gives the *Spirit* without limit. (Jn. 3:34)

The Spirit and the words of God belong together. Again,

> The *Spirit* gives life; the flesh counts for nothing. The *words* that I have spoken to you are spirit and they are life. (Jn. 6:63)

Again:

> But you will receive power when the Holy Spirit has come on you; and you will be my witnesses in Jerusalem, and in all Judea and Samaria, and to the ends of the earth. (Acts 1:8)

What will happen with the coming of the Spirit? The disciples will bear witness to Jesus. They will speak the gospel. See this happening in Acts 5:30–32:

> The God of our fathers raised Jesus from the dead – whom you killed by hanging him on a tree. God exalted him to his own right hand as Prince and Saviour that he might give repentance and forgiveness of sins to Israel. We are witnesses of these things, and so is the Holy Spirit, whom God has given to those who obey him.

The gospel they preach is not only their testimony, but the testimony of the Holy Spirit, the breath of God. Consider Paul's words to the Thessalonians:

> For we know, brothers loved by God, that he has chosen you; because our gospel came to you not simply with words, but also with power, with the Holy Spirit and with deep conviction. You know how we lived among you for your sake. You became imitators of us and of the Lord; in spite of severe suffering, you welcomed the message with the joy given by the Holy Spirit (1 Thes. 1:4–6)

Paul is describing one experience, what they experienced when 'our gospel came'. The gospel is never just words. Exactly the same point is made in the next chapter:

> And we also thank God continually because, when you received the word of God, which you heard from us, you accepted it not as the word of men, but as it actually is, the word of God, which is at work in you who believe. (1 Thes. 2:13)

The gospel comes in power and in the Holy Spirit precisely because it is the Word *of God*. Notice, too, that Paul says that this Word of God is at work 'in you who believe'. Paul can equally say that God is at work 'in us' by his Spirit. These are not two works of God, but one. It is by his Word that God's Spirit is at work. We will understand the living Word of God in the New Testament, and in our lives, only when we see the inseparable connection between God's Spirit and God's Word, God's breath and God's speech – when we see, as Paul puts it in Ephesians 6:17, that the sword of the Spirit is the Word of God.

It is not surprising, then, that there are many statements in the New Testament where 'Spirit' and 'Word' are virtually interchangeable. The concept of the new birth is a case in point. When James says that God 'chose to give us birth through the word of truth' (Jas. 1:18), would he have been saying something very different if he had said, 'God chose to give us birth through his Spirit'? Peter says: 'You have been born again, not of perishable seed, but of imperishable, through the living and enduring word of God . . .' (1 Pet. 1:23). Is he speaking of something different from what Jesus describes: 'I tell you the truth, no-one can enter the kingdom of heaven unless he is born of water and the Spirit' (Jn. 3:5).

Jesus said of the Holy Spirit: 'When he comes, he will convict the world of guilt in regard to sin and righteousness and judgment: in regard to sin, because men do not believe in me; in regard to righteousness, because I am going to the Father, where you can see me no longer; and in regard to judgment, because the prince of this world now stands condemned' (Jn. 16:8–11). Was he speaking of something other than what would happen through the proclamation of the gospel? The Spirit is the Spirit of *truth* (Jn. 16:13) who will lead us into all truth, and this truth is the gospel – as Jesus said, 'he will testify about me' (Jn. 15:26).

Christian thought about the work of the Spirit has too often been separated from the Word of God. This is the result of an inadequate understanding of the 'living' nature of the Word of God. The Spirit tends to be seen in anything that we do not understand, anything that is irrational, anything that is *different from* the effect of God's Word. Inner convictions are said to be the work of the Spirit – especially if we cannot explain them in any other way. Strange phenomena, particularly heightened emotional, paranormal, or even orgiastic experiences are attributed to the Spirit, simply because they are strange.

Consider, however, Romans 8:16: 'The Spirit himself testifies with our spirit that we are God's children.' Like many New Testament statements, this refers to the subjective *effect* of the Spirit's work. Subjective experience (in the sense of personal and individual experience of which one is the subject, but not in the sense of introspective experience) is certainly important in the Christian life. The question, however, remains – *how* does the Spirit testify to me? The answer is, surely, by the gospel, by the Word of God. Are there *two* experiences, the Word of God telling me that I am a child of God, and the Spirit testifying with my spirit that I am a child of God? No. God's Word comes with the power of God's Spirit. God himself breathes his Word to me. Receiving the *breath* of God and the *words* of God are not distinguishable experiences here.

Evangelicals have often failed to understand this, and in effect have believed in two sources of revelation. This criticism was levelled at the sixteenth-century Reformers. According to the Roman Catholics, the Reformers had simply replaced the twin authorities of Scripture and tradition with Scripture and the subjective testimony of the Spirit. Catholic theology would reason as follows: 'How do I know the Bible is God's Word? The church tells me.' Why is it better, they asked, to say 'I know it in my heart'? How can you be more certain that the testimony in your heart, rather than the testimony of God's church, is the work of God's Spirit?

I believe, however (although it is a matter of debate), that these critics had misunderstood the Reformers. The Reformers were not speaking about two revelations from God, one objective in the Bible (saying, for example, 'Jesus Christ is Lord'), and another subjective in our hearts (saying, 'The Bible is *my* Word'). Rather, they were saying that the objective Word that Jesus is Lord comes with the power of God's Spirit, exactly because it is the Word *of God*. God *breathes* that Word to me, and by it brings about faith in him, just as he did with Abraham. It is one work, not two:

> For God, who said, 'Let light shine out of darkness,' made his light shine in our hearts to give us the light of the knowledge of the glory of God in the face of Christ. (2 Cor. 4:6).

That is the work of God's Spirit; it is the work of the gospel Word.

Conclusion

It remains to spell out the connection between the living Word and preaching. When Paul writes, 'All Scripture is *God-breathed* and useful for teaching, rebuking, correcting and training in righteousness . . .' (2 Tim. 3:16), he is referring more directly to the present function of Scripture than to its origin. While there are implications for our understanding of the origin of Scripture, the context suggests that Scripture is the Word which God 'breathes out' today. This is how the writer of Hebrews understood the matter (*e.g.* Heb. 3:7), and it is the understanding of Scripture reflected in Jesus words, 'Have you not read what God said *to you?*' (Mt. 22:31). Precisely for this reason Scripture is profitable for teaching, rebuking, correcting and training in righteousness: it is the Word that God himself speaks today. Therefore the surest way to recover the preaching of the 'living' Word of God is to recover preaching that truly expounds the Scriptures.

The call that Dick Lucas has consistently issued, and the immense help that he has given, to preachers to expound the Scriptures faithfully is nothing less than a summons to preach the *living* Word. This calls for humility and confidence: humility in prayer and study because it is God who breathes his Word to men and women as the Scriptures are expounded; confidence in the task, because his Word will accomplish his purpose (Is. 55:11).

Notes

1. Much of the material in this essay was first prepared at Dick Lucas' invitation for the Evangelical Ministry Assembly in 1989. I remain much in debt to Dick Lucas for his invitation and encouragement to explore these matters, as well as for his generous fellowship on various occasions then and since.

2. See extensive references to Luther's writings on this subject in Regin Prenter, *Spiritus Creator*, trans. John M. Jensen (Philadelphia: Fortress, 1953), pp. 101–130. It is often said that Luther believed that 'it is the Spirit who makes the letter of Scripture into the Word of God, which is for that reason the living presence of Christ in us. He is the word': Yves Congar, *The Word and the Spirit* (London: Geoffrey Chapman; San Francisco: Harper and Row, 1986), trans. David Smith from *La Parole et le Souffle* (Paris: Desclée, 1984), p. 127, note 3.

3. See Walter Kreck, 'Parole et Esprit selon Calvin', *Revue d'histoire et de philosophie religieuses* 40 (1960), pp. 213–228. Also Jan Veenhof, 'The Holy Spirit and Hermeneutics', in *The Challenge of Evangelical Theology: Essays in Approach and Method*, ed. Nigel M. de S. Cameron (Edinburgh: Rutherford House Books, 1987), pp. 118–119.

4. See, *e.g.*, the Roman Catholic writer Yves Congar, *op. cit.*

5. See, *e.g.*, Paul Helm, 'Faith, Evidence, and the Scriptures', in *Scripture and Truth*, ed. D. A. Carson and John D. Woodbridge (Leicester: IVP, 1983), pp. 312–313, on the relation between the power of the Scriptures to speak and the 'inner testimony of the Spirit'; Geoffrey W. Bromiley, 'The Church Fathers and Holy Scripture', in *Scripture and Truth*, p. 214, on the Church Fathers' understanding of the role of the Spirit in the understanding of Scripture; John D. Woodbridge and Randall H. Balmer, 'The Princetonians and Biblical Authority', in *Scripture and Truth*, pp. 269–271, on the importance of the Holy Spirit for the doctrine of Scripture of the Princetonians, especially Charles Hodge and A. A. Hodge: 'We recognize the Bible's authority because of the confirming witness of the Holy Spirit within us' (*ibid.*, p. 269); John M. Frame, 'The Spirit and the Scriptures', in *Hermeneutics, Authority and Canon*, ed. D. A. Carson and John D. Woodbridge (Leicester: IVP, 1986), pp. 213–235; J. I. Packer, *God Has Spoken*, revised edition (London: Hodder and Stoughton, 1979), pp. 132–133, on the necessity for Bible readers to be open to the working of the Spirit. None of these discussions develops the intimate relationship between Word and Spirit that is on view in this paper.

6. Compare the use of the verb here translated 'credited' in Gn. 50:20; Jb. 13:24; 19:11; 33:10.

7. Note Paul's words to the Corinthians urging them to 'consider your call' (1 Cor. 1:26, RSV).

4

Preaching the whole Bible

Preaching and biblical theology

Peter F. Jensen

Imagine that you have decided to preach through Matthew's gospel. Here is the gateway to the New Testament, the place at which the ordinary reader will begin. At once you are faced with the sort of difficulty which leads many preachers to prefer Mark or Luke or John. Matthew begins his gospel in a most unattractive way, with the genealogy of Jesus (Mt. 1:1–17). You are confronted not with an open and inviting gateway to the New Testament, but with a locked and gloomy portal, forbidding to all but the most persistent.

What should you do if Matthew is on the preaching syllabus? Emulating Superman, you may take a mighty bound over these seventeen verses and find yourself in the green and pleasant pastures of the Christmas story. Matthew's gospel can now begin in earnest. You should, however, have a somewhat uneasy conscience. How can you claim to expound the Scriptures if you are so selective? How can you tell the whole story when omitting parts?

In fact, Matthew's genealogy can and should be expounded as a vital element of Matthew's gospel. It reminds both the reader and the preacher that the world they are entering is not exactly the same as their own, and that it has different values and different ways of doing things. Even more important, it is also a reminder that here is a world with a history, and that Jesus Christ is born not into a randomly chosen family or nation, but into a select family of a select nation. If our business as preachers is to proclaim Christ, his family history is a vital part of that proclamation.

Thus the New Testament itself confronts the expository preacher with a sharp choice. Will I expound the whole Bible or will I select certain parts of it and leave others to one side? To what extent will I make it my aim 'to proclaim to you the whole will of God' as Paul did among the Ephesians (Acts 20:27)?

Some ministers occupy the same pulpit for long enough to preach sermons on all the chapters of the Bible. This, however, is not what is meant by 'preaching the whole Bible'. *The goal of 'preaching the whole Bible' is attained when we so preach Christ that every part of the Bible contributes its unique riches to his gospel.* Just as Jesus himself drew on the Law of Moses, the Prophets and the Psalms (Lk. 24:44), so we will incorporate every part of the Bible in our teaching, whether psalm or narrative, letter or apocalypse, proverb or law. The whole gospel of Christ is made up by the diversity of the Bible; the diversity of the Bible is summed up in the gospel of Christ. To be selective in our preaching is to diminish Christ; our aim is to proclaim the whole Christ in the whole Bible.

Such is the goal. Few, however, aspire to achieve it. Many preachers are inhibited by the difficulties I am about to describe. They are content to dwell on the familiar and the apparently straightforward. They give the Christmas story without the genealogy, not realizing that the genealogy is integral to the story. As a result, they do not preach Christ in all his glory, and both for them and for their listeners the Bible appears to consist of a series of unconnected segments without a central unifying theme. Even worse is the case of those who Christianize the Old Testament by the simple device of preaching about Jesus from every passage, often with the aid of allegory. It is my contention that the task of preaching the whole Bible can be accomplished only with the aid of a robust biblical theory. From such a theology the preacher will gain a sense of the whole, with a capacity to do justice to the parts.

Hindrances to preaching the whole Bible

There are grave hindrances which inhibit the preaching of the whole Bible. If preachers are to develop sufficient confidence to preach Christ through the whole scope of the biblical revelation, we must recognize what these problems are. There are difficulties which arise from the nature of the Bible; there are difficulties connected to the modern reader; and there are difficulties posed by the education of the preacher.

The Bible itself

It is first and foremost the nature of the Bible which constitutes a barrier to extensive expository preaching. Many parts of the Bible (especially elements of the Old Testament) are obscure and difficult for modern audiences to understand. A whole world of religion, of language, of custom and of technology separates us. Very few in any urban audience of today have ever seen an animal sacrifice (for example), or have the power to imagine what it was like. Likewise, whereas the prophetic words galvanized their first audiences, the very fact of their original relevance makes them distant to us. To take another case, the ancient food laws seem arbitrary and even bizarre. Conversely, many parts of the Bible (especially elements of the New Testament) are clear, powerful and attractive. One can spend a ministry expounding them without having to turn to the parts which seem difficult and obscure.

Some of the literature of Scripture is difficult to relate to the main thrust of the Bible. Bible-reading becomes akin to the study of an unfamiliar Shakespearian play. The text is studded with brilliant aphorisms calling out to be quoted. But the cast of characters is huge and hard to remember, the line of thought in long speeches is too complex to follow easily, and the plot is grasped only in a hazy way. You could give an excellent address based on a clever aphorism, but where these words fit into the whole play may not be clear to you or to your hearers. Indeed, you may unintentionally commend an attitude completely at odds with that of the author.

Parts of the Scriptures seem to lack moral or spiritual value. They fall below the standards of the Sermon on the Mount or 1 Corinthians 13, and may be better left in deepest darkness shrouded. Various chapters in the book of Judges seem ideal as a means of entertaining ten-year-old boys at a camp; they are likely to cause affront or bewilderment among contemporary adults. Some of the psalms are notoriously vengeful. Likewise, some sections of Scripture are not especially well written, and tend to be boring. They do not directly feed the spiritual life; should we preach on them when so much else is magnificent?

Much of the problem can be summed up by saying that the relationship between the parts of the Bible and the whole of the Bible is unclear. For many, the Bible is merely an anthology of writings, something like an *Oxford Book of Religion*, with good and bad parts but no coherent message. Indeed, the Old Testament constitutes the gravest difficulty. It is true that the Old Testament has its gems and the New Testament has its problems, but overall it is the Old Testament which is the problem. Can a way be found to enable the parts of Scripture to contribute to the whole, and the illumination of the whole to help explain the parts?

The readers of the Bible

If the Bible has its difficulties, they have been worsened by the inadequate preparation given to today's readers of the Bible.

There is biblical illiteracy even in the churches. The emphasis on the Sunday eucharist and lectionary preaching is in part responsible for this, but there are many other reasons. Personal Bible-reading is superficial or not engaged in at all, and most people do not hear exposition in their churches. As with all things, ignorance is compounded; the less we know, the less we know. The poor in knowledge get poorer. Conversely, however, acquaintance with the whole Bible continually reinforces itself, as allusions, parallels, types, and symbols begin to be recognized.

The generally accepted methods of instructing children create a false expectation. Not surprisingly, the staple of instruction is the Bible story, plucked seemingly at random from the Bible. Children (and therefore adults) are left with the overwhelming impression that the Bible is an encyclopedia of unconnected and episodic material told for the purpose of providing moral and spiritual guidance. It is only necessary to test the average congregation of adults at a superficial level to discover the appalling lack of any sense that the Bible has an overall significance, that its parts connect. The absence of any knowledge of the history covered in the Bible (let alone the development of revelation) is distressing. I say nothing of the ignorance of doctrine which has been banished from both classroom and pulpit for many years past.

The moralistic use of Scripture in so many pulpits distorts the reader's understanding of Scripture. I once heard a preacher explain that the accident which led to the lameness of Mephibosheth (2 Sa. 4:4) was given in Scripture to warn parents to be careful in carrying their children. After all, it was reasoned, Scripture must mean something and have some application to behaviour. In the absence of any thematic treatment of books and a thematic treatment of Scripture as a whole, such solecisms are inevitable.

The preparation of preachers

The most significant hindrance to the preaching of the whole Bible, however, is the problem posed by contemporary theological education. The problem has a twofold root: first, the dominance of liberal presuppositions over evangelical presuppositions in the treatment of Scripture, and secondly, evangelical defensiveness.

David Kelsey has depicted the distinction between the two presuppositional attitudes in a revealing way.

> In a third-century AD pagan or Christian academy, one might study ancient texts so as to become more deeply shaped by the virtues . . . In a research university one studies ancient texts to research the truth about them, their origins, their meanings in their original settings, the history of their uses, the history of teaching about them or readings of them, perhaps the social or psychological dynamics that explain why such texts come to be written.[1]

As Kelsey shows, the first attitude dominated the treatment of Scripture until the Enlightenment. Clearly its approach is not uncritical, and just as clearly the second approach may be accompanied by a desire to receive God's Word. But the distinction is fundamental, and when evangelical scholars accept the critical presuppositions, they cease to be evangelical in their doctrine of Scripture, although their personal piety may be for some time relatively unaffected.

It is true, of course, that many evangelical scholars do not accept the liberal presuppositions. But they have become defensive. Much of their work is dedicated to demonstrating the validity of conservative conclusions about the Bible in terms dictated by the research university. Valuable though this is, it has not been sufficiently accompanied by the setting forth of the theology of the Bible taken as a whole. The preachers of God's Word are persuaded about its truth, but deficient in preaching Christ from the whole of God's unified revelation. The agenda continues to be set by academic liberalism. Students have been left with the impression that the Bible is a critical minefield. We have created uncertainty rather than strengthening faith. We need to develop a coherent account of the whole Bible which will enable its message to be preached with confidence. In short, we need a biblical theology.

The basis of biblical theology

As David Kelsey reminds us, the basis of academic theology is critical history, researching the text. Such an approach is presuppositionally incapable of creating a biblical theology. 'Biblical' is itself a suspect category on two grounds. First, it suggests that the sixty-six books belong together in a unity which enables a common theology to be constructed. But the Bible is said to be marked by variety and contradiction. Secondly, it suggests that there can be an authorized canon of literature, whereas the choice of these books is said to be arbitrary, needing to be supplemented by other Israelite and Christian texts. Not surprisingly the enterprise of 'biblical theology', although it was undertaken with some zeal during the middle decades of the twentieth century, has largely fallen into disrepute.[2]

Evangelicals, however, have a view of Scripture which not only enables the development of biblical theory, but demands it. The basis of this view is that the Bible is the product of the Lord who speaks. Indeed, the Lord himself is both the author and the content of Scripture. Three results are entailed by this evangelical conviction.

First, *the Bible is one in origin and content.* Scripture is unique in its origin. Without doubt it has been shaped by many human hands; without doubt it bears the marks of the different personalities whom the Lord inspired to write his words; without doubt there is a great variety of literature, of historical background, of perspective in its pages. But when all these observations have been given their due weight, it remains true that there is a fundamental unity to the Bible, a unity which arises from its origin in the mind of God. The Lord is both its author and its content. The inspiration of the Bible gives it, furthermore, a unique authority. The Lord who is the content of Scripture is the creator, the ruler and the saviour. He rules his people through his Word, the Bible.

Secondly, *the Bible is God's revelation of himself.* The unity of the Bible is not only a unity of origin but also a unity of subject matter. From first to last it is centred on the Lord God, his words, his deeds, his plans. He is the content of Scripture. The greatest of the Bible's human actors is Jesus Christ who is the Lord himself, both God and man. It is true that the Bible tells us more than any other book about ourselves and how we should believe and behave. But the central focus remains the Lord, and what it tells us about ourselves can be understood only in that context.

Thirdly, *the Bible interprets the Bible.* No human interpreter, ecclesiastical or academic, can be allowed to stand in final judgment on the Word of the Lord who speaks. However much we may be aided by human interpreters, the key to all interpretation necessarily remains the comparison of Scripture with Scripture. A good cross-reference system remains one of the best commentaries on Scripture; there is no substitute for a thorough knowledge of the whole Bible in theological education.[3] If the Bible is God's Word, the whole Bible is the ultimate context of any part of it. If our knowledge of the whole is defective, we will not understand the part; if we are ignorant of the part, we cannot know the whole.

The nature of biblical theology

As the Lord is one, so the Bible is one, and this is the impetus for biblical theology. Two complementary methods of approach to the Bible can justly claim the name of biblical theology, although I intend to distinguish them for the sake of discussion and use the name only of the second. Both are needed for preaching the whole Bible.

First, there is a *topical* approach to Scripture. By the study of the text it becomes apparent that certain topics are frequently referred to, and a picture of revealed truth about these subjects becomes clear. We can relate what the Bible has to say about the Spirit, about the death of Jesus, about the last things, and about humanity, for example. In due course the Bible's teaching on these subjects can be integrated to some extent, and so a biblical theology can be arrived at. It is the foundation and chief part of systematic theology, but systematic theology also draws on historical and contemporary theology. The task of creating a doctrinal theology of this sort depends upon careful exegesis of the texts of Scripture. In accordance with the unity of Scripture, however, such biblical theology also assists with exegesis. It is a method of comparing Scripture with Scripture. The development of such a theology assists the preacher to focus on what is important in Scripture and guard against idiosyncratic interpretations.

Secondly, there is a *thematic* approach to Scripture. In this case the study of the text is carried through chronologically. It is a study of the development of the themes of Scripture as they unfold in the narrative of Scripture itself. It begins with exegesis; it incorporates the theologies of the various books and authors of Scripture; it is basic to systematic doctrinal theology; it is centred on Jesus Christ; and it is essential to grasp if one intends to preach on the whole Bible. Without it, topical study is in danger of arbitrary 'proof-texting'. It is the thematic approach that I wish to identify specifically as biblical theology, pressing home the need for its incorporation in the preacher's equipment. Many preachers are exegetically able and doctrinally informed, but they lack the intermediate discipline of biblical theology.

Various authors have described such a biblical theology.[4] Professor John Murray called it 'that branch of Exegetical Theology which deals with the process of the self-revelation of God deposited in the Bible'.[5] D. A. Carson offers a slightly different definition: 'that branch of theology whose concern it is to study each corpus of the Scripture in its own right, especially with respect to its place in the history of God's unfolding revelation. The emphasis is on history and the individual corpus.'[6]

Graeme Goldsworthy has written a fine introduction to biblical theology. It is intended for lay people but it would repay study by all who preach God's Word. He speaks of his subject in these terms:

> Biblical theology is concerned with God's saving acts and his word as these occur within the history of the people of God.

It follows the progress of revelation from the first word of God to man through to the unveiling of the full glory of Christ. It examines the several stages of biblical history and their relationship to one another. It thus provides the basis for understanding how texts in one part of the Bible relate to all other texts. A sound interpretation of the Bible is based upon the findings of biblical theology.[7]

It is Goldsworthy's description that is closest to my view of the meaning and shape of biblical theology.[8]

The content of biblical theology

The construction of a biblical theology is obviously the study of a lifetime. All that I can do here is to introduce the subject in broad terms, with no attempt to engage in a technical or academic discussion. Like all theological work, my introduction is open to challenge and revision in the light of Scripture itself.

Four features of biblical theology are prominent. They flow from our central conviction that the Lord is both the author and content of Scripture, and that the Bible is the product of the Lord who speaks.

First, *the biblical revelation has a framework*. At a fundamental level, four great 'moments' are evident – creation, fall, salvation and consummation. The story of the third of these, salvation, dominates the Bible, and has its own structure; but creation, fall and consummation provide the essential framework within which the history of salvation unfolds. The passages of Scripture that describe creation, fall and consummation are relatively brief in extent, but highly significant in content.

Secondly, *the biblical revelation has a main theme*. Put most simply, the theme of Scripture is the kingdom of God, by which I mean the rule of God through his Word. From the doctrine of creation we see that God is the supreme Lord, master and creator of all things by the sheer power of his Word. In his world and over his world he places humankind. Adam and Eve rule the world, but are themselves ruled by the Word of God. In creation, God's kingdom is established.

From the doctrine of the fall we see that the problems of the human race are caused by rebellion against our rightful Lord. Since the Lord rules by his Word, it is specifically his Word which is doubted and disobeyed. Likewise, it is the Word of God that stands over humankind in judgment and promise as Adam and Eve are expelled from Eden. In the fall, God's kingdom is challenged.

From the doctrine of the consummation, we see that the glory of God is to be vindicated and the problems of the human race are to be resolved as God's children submit to him as king and as he dwells in their midst as sovereign Lord once more. All this will fulfil the promise of his Word. In the consummation, God's kingdom has come.

What of the theme of God's kingdom in the doctrine of salvation? It is no accident that the burden of Jesus' preaching was the announcement of God's kingdom, or that Paul summarized his gospel as 'Jesus Christ as Lord' (2 Cor. 4:5). Throughout the Bible, God summons his people to submit to his kingdom, to place themselves under his Word once again, and so be saved. Three elements of the Word of the Lord are especially relevant to the task of describing biblical theology.

1. The Lord's Word was frequently formalized in terms of covenants. A covenant was especially suitable for the establishment of relationships, particularly where the submission of one party to another is involved. The essence of a covenant is promise and the necessary response to a covenant is faith. Covenants can take different forms, making no demands (for example), or being accompanied by extensive stipulations. But in any case, they contain promise and faith and they function to establish relationships.

2. The relationships established by covenant help to form the history and patterns of salvation. This is especially true of the covenants with Noah (Gn. 9), with Abraham (Gn. 12, 15), with Israel through Moses (Ex. 19 – 24), with David (2 Sa. 7) and through Christ (Mt. 26:28). It is worth noting that some covenants reflect different forms of being God's people, whether as family, as nation, as monarchy, or as church. The connection between the covenants is also an important study, as we consider how they lead into one another. In the final analysis, however, there is but one covenant, as there is one Lord and Saviour, and one kingdom of God.

3. God's ruling Word is not, however, always formalized as covenant. The knowledge needed by his people to live obediently in the created world came in different ways. For example, the wisdom literature of Scripture, found in books such as Proverbs, Psalms, Ecclesiastes and Job, addresses questions raised by the presence of God's kingdom in the world in ways which the other literature cannot. Not all of ethics can be encapsulated in the legal form; a wisdom literature is needed to delineate wise and foolish behaviour as well. But the Proverbs begin with the same assumption as the rest of the Bible, that the fear of the Lord is the beginning of wisdom, and that the Word of the Lord is the ruling principle of human existence.

Thirdly, *the biblical revelation has a structure*. The most basic distinction which every Bible reader immediately recognizes is that between Old and New Testaments. This division corresponds to the absolute significance of Jesus Christ in the biblical scheme of things. So significant is his coming, so great is the watershed, that the old is not able to contain it; it is surpassed as the sun surpasses the moon in glory and splendour: 'In the past God spoke to our forefathers through the prophets at many times and in various ways, but in these last days he has spoken to us by his Son . . .' (Heb. 1:1–2). One of the chief tasks of biblical theology is to discern where the new differs from the old.

As the letter to the Hebrews reminds us, however, the Son who is this last great Word of God is understood only through the categories of the old covenant. There is discontinuity, but there is continuity; there is disjunction, but there is harmony; there is diversity, but there is unity. For the same God is Lord both of the old and of the new, and he has provided in the pattern and promises of the old the very language and copies of the new: 'The law is only a shadow of the good things that are coming – not the realities themselves' (Heb. 10:1).

Within the Old Testament there is diversity, but there is also a unified forward movement as the theme of God's kingdom is developed. As we preach 'the whole Bible', we need to be aware of the context of each passage within the flow of that history, what it is linked to and what it reveals about the nature and purposes of the Lord. We will take a passage on its own terms, giving careful attention to exegesis and to its place in the book in which it appears. But we will not fail to consider the wider questions, too. Is there elsewhere in Scripture another passage which bears on this one by way of supplement or contrast? More especially, what contribution does this passage bring to the whole story of creation, fall, salvation and consummation? Where does it fit in the unfolding of the history of redemption? What does it contribute to our knowledge of the main theme of Scripture, the kingdom of God through his Word, culminating in Jesus Christ?

In all this, the study of the covenants is most helpful. Promises are always future-looking, and hence the covenants help to provide the forward impetus of the biblical revelation. The prophetic author of 1 Kings rejoices to describe the reign of Solomon in terms which fulfil the covenant with Abraham (1 Ki. 4:20–21), with Moses (8:56–61), and with David (8:24–26). But he describes also the collapse of these earthly fulfilments, and would doubtless join with the prophet Isaiah in looking for a transformed and renewed day of Davidic empire (Is. 11). Thus the Old Testament, despite its riches of spiritual insight into the human relationship with God, is essentially unfulfilled and forward-looking. Although we must firmly repudiate the simplistic practice of referring to Jesus in every sermon, there is no doubt that he is the hermeneutical key to the Scriptures, since he is the one in whom 'every one of God's promises is a "Yes"' (2 Cor. 1:20, NRSV).

Within the New Testament there is also a structure, though of a different sort. In this case the promise nature of biblical religion has created a special eschatological moment. We exist in the period between the ages, the period of the kingdom which has come and is yet to come. Furthermore, the existing promises of God are seen to have come true in Christ, but they have been transformed and transcended. We justly describe Christ in terms of the old, and the old is described in terms of Christ. But it is a new temple, a new priesthood, a king who rules at the cross and in heaven, a land which is above, the sacrifice of a person, and a church which is no longer also a nation. The crucial point is to follow the New Testament interpretation of the Old Testament. When we do, we can 'preach the whole Bible', and so preach the biblical Christ.

Finally, *the biblical revelation has a pattern and a language.* The story of salvation describes the deeds of the Lord with his people. In the Old Testament era, the Lord's acts are often those by which he saves his people from the threatening forces of natural chaos and military opposition. At the same time, since he is a righteous Lord, his people experience his wrath, as their disobedience is met with punishment. The Lord is a judge who both confounds and delivers. In these acts he reveals his character and purposes and there is a consistency in his deeds which enables his prophets to describe the present and future in terms of the past.

From this consistency there emerges therefore both a pattern and a vocabulary by which the New Testament understands the work of Christ. Thus the exodus from Egypt is linked with the exodus which Christ accomplished in Jerusalem, and helps to explain it (Lk. 8:30–31). When Paul speaks of what Christ has done, he uses both the story and the language of the exodus: 'he has rescued us from the dominion of darkness and brought us into the kingdom of the Son he loves, in whom we have redemption, the forgiveness of sins' (Col. 1:13–14).

In this connection, one of the most illuminating passages in the New Testament is the speech of James to the Jerusalem council in Acts 15. The issue was, of course, the terms by which Gentile believers were to to admitted into the privilege of salvation (15:5). Barnabas and Paul had spoken of what God had done among the Gentiles through them, using the phrase 'signs and wonders', which is part of the Old Testament vocabulary of redemption (Ex. 7:3). James then appealed to Amos and took up a passage in which the prophet foreshadowed the re-establishment of the empire of David (Am. 9:11–12). He did not take these words to predict the literal resurrection of David's political kingdom. For him, the coming of the Gentiles into the kingdom of Christ was their fulfilment. The original prophecy was transformed and transcended by this marvellous result. In so doing he provides us with a clue to the Bible's own treatment of the promises and their completion in Christ. This is how Scripture interprets Scripture, with Christ the Lord as the hermeneutical key.

Conclusion

At the beginning of this essay, I indicated some of the hindrances to preaching the whole Bible. I have argued that the development of a biblical theology is essential to dealing with these problems. Biblical theology will make sense of the unity and the diversity of Scripture and enable the preacher to emphasize what really matters. It is in the light of the whole of what the Bible teaches about God's judgment, for example, that the contribution of Judges or the Psalms needs to be assessed. Likewise, the sacrificial system is both illumined by, and illuminating of, the atoning death of Christ. The food laws should be read in connection with the problem of the Jews and the Gentiles in the New Testament. Moralism will be avoided as we place passages in the wider context of the advance of God's kingdom.

A theologian once said to me that he never heard sermons about God. It was obvious at once that he could not be consistently receiving expository preaching of the whole Bible shaped by biblical theology. Such preaching will not neglect the application of the Bible to its human audience, but it will of necessity focus on who God is, what he has done, what he is doing and what he will do. It will have Jesus Christ at its centre and the kingdom of God as its theme. We attain the goal of 'preaching the whole Bible' when we so preach Christ that every part of the Bible contributes its unique riches to his gospel. When we fail to preach like this, we diminish Christ; when we preach like this, we give him his whole glory.

Notes

1. David H. Kelsey, *To Understand God Truly* (Philadelphia: Westminster, 1992), p. 85.

2. There has been, of course, the interesting development of 'canonical criticism', but the theological undergirding of this enterprise remains vulnerable to critical attack.

3. Surely evangelicals will not remain content with the short time currently devoted to theological education, and with the crowding out of Scripture study in favour of other, less important, matters.

4. I am aware, of course, of the history of the term 'biblical theology' with its initial use to distinguish it from dogmatic theology. Details of the history can be found in the standard dictionaries. But I do not wish to be diverted from discussing what an evangelical theology of Scripture may produce by way of biblical theology.

5. Quoted by R. B. Gaffin Jr, 'Systematic Theology and Biblical Theology', *Westminster Theological Journal* 3 (1976), p. 288. Gaffin's article is a valuable contribution to this subject.

6. D. A. Carson and J. D. Woodbridge (eds.), *Scripture and Truth* (Leicester:

IVP, 1983), p. 69.

7. G. Goldsworthy, *According to Plan* (Leicester: IVP, 1991), p. 37.

8. Other material for biblical theology includes G. Vos, *Biblical Theology* (Grand Rapids: Eerdmans, 1948), W. J. Dumbrell, *Creation and Covenant* (Exeter: Paternoster, 1984); D. W. B. Robinson, *Faith's Framework* (Exeter: Paternoster, 1985).

5

Preaching Christ from the Old Testament Scriptures

Sinclair B. Ferguson

The discipline of biblical theology has slowly but surely found a place in evangelical preaching.[1] As a result, it has now become a commonplace in the teaching of homiletics to stress that we must preach Christ *in all the Scriptures* in a manner that takes account of the flow of redemptive history. In particular we must learn to preach Christ from the Old Testament without falling into the old traps of an artificial exegesis.

But how do we legitimately preach the text of the Old Testament as those who stand on this side of Pentecost? What difference does it make to expound Genesis or Psalms as believers in Jesus Christ? Or, to put it in a more graphic way, how can we reconstruct the principles of Jesus' conversation in Luke 24:25–27 and 45, and learn to follow his example of showing how all the Scriptures point to him so that hearts are 'strangely warmed' and begin to burn? In particular, how may we do this without lapsing into what we (sometimes a little too cavalierly) deem to be either patristic allegorizing or post-reformation spiritualizing? If only we had heard how Jesus did this on the Emmaus Road, in the Upper Room, during the forty days between his resurrection and his ascension, we might grasp the principles by which it is done, so that we too could genuinely preach the text of the Old Testament as Christian preachers and not as rabbis!

Yet we must also preach the Scriptures without denuding them of the genuine historical events they record and the reality of the personal experiences they describe or to which they were originally addressed. How, then, do we preach Christ, and him crucified without leapfrogging over these historical realities as though the Old Testament Scriptures had no real significance for their own historical context?

In discussing the pre-Christ revelation of God as trinity, B. B. Warfield describes the Old Testament as a richly furnished but dimly lit room. Only when the light is turned on do the contents become clear. That light has been switched on in Christ and in the New Testament's testimony to him. Now the triune personal being of God becomes clear.[2] To read the Old Testament with the light switched off would be to deny the historical reality of our own context. On the other hand, we would be denying the historical reality of the text and its context if we were to read and preach it as though that same light had already been switched on within its own pages. Thus our task as Christian preachers must be to take account of both. Fulfilling that task drives us back into the basic hermeneutical question for the Christian exegete: how do we relate the Old Testament to the New Testament? The longer we labour in ministry, the more we ask that question. The more we know about the answer to it, the more we realize there is so much more left to explore. It is a life-long pursuit. Here we can make only a few comments and suggest some principles that are generally applicable and may be specifically helpful to the preacher.

Preaching Christ must become instinctive, not formulaic

Young preachers are often told, 'You must preach *Christ* from the Old Testament.' But having just finished preaching on (for example) Psalm 121, and realizing that we have said little or nothing about Jesus (perhaps not explicitly mentioned his name!), we may be in great agitation, and search desperately for a magic formula that will help us to preach Christ from the Old Testament.

It would be possible, of course, to provide a kind of formula, a kind of homiletical version of Thomas's five ways, such as: point to Christ by showing: (1) the passage is a direct prophecy of him; or (2) the passage shows why Jesus is needed; or (3) the passage speaks about something that reminds us of Jesus; or (4) the passage speaks about something that could not be accomplished without Jesus; or (5) the passage shows us an individual/group unlike Jesus.

The point here is not to comment on whether or not these five ways are helpful so much as the inherent danger in the approach. It is likely to produce preaching that is wooden and insensitive to the rich contours of biblical theology. Its artificiality would lie in our going through the motions of exegeting and expounding the Old Testament and then, remembering the formula, tidying our notes in order to align them with it. The net result over an extended period of time might be akin to that produced by sermons for children: the intelligent child soon recognizes that the answer to the minister's questions will always be one of the following: God; Jesus; Sin; the Bible; Be Good!

Of course we need to work with general principles as we develop as preachers; but it is a far greater desideratum that we develop an instinctive mindset and, corresponding to that, such a passion for Jesus Christ himself that we will find our way to him in a natural and realistic manner rather than a merely formulaic one.

This is a much bigger issue than how we preach Christ from the Old Testament, for at least two reasons. First, because (if my own assessment is correct) many sermons from the *Gospels* – where the focus is explicitly on the person of Jesus – are far from Christ-centred, never mind sermons from the Old Testament.

How is this possible? The preacher has looked into the text principally to find himself and his congregation, not to find Christ. The sermon is consequently about 'people in the Gospels' rather than about Jesus Christ who is the gospel. The real question the preacher has been interested in asking and answering, is not 'How do we find *Christ* in this Gospel?' but 'Where am *I* in this story? What have *I* got to do?' Even though an entire series of such sermons on a Gospel is preached (as in the *lectio continua* method), we will not necessarily have communicated the basic life of Jesus. Instead we have been given an exploration of the human condition.

So there is a confused mindset here that raises a deeper question than 'Is there a formula that helps us to preach Christ from the Old Testament?' The more fundamental issue is the question, 'What am I really looking for when I am preaching on *any* part of the Bible? Am I really looking to tell people what they are like and what they must do – that is, am I really stressing the subjective and the imperative – or am I talking about Jesus Christ himself and the gospel? Do I stress the objective and the indicative of the gospel in the light of which the subjective and imperative are to be considered? After all, it is not the subjective (my condition) or the imperative (respond!) that saves or transforms people's lives, but the objective and the indicative of God's grace received subjectively in the light of the imperatives of the gospel.

In evangelicalism at large there has been a Schleiermacher-like retreat into the subjective. Luther's *bon mot* that the gospel is 'entirely outside of us' has become an axiom strange to our ears. It badly needs to be recovered.

A second observation worth noting in this connection is that many (perhaps most) outstanding preachers of the Bible (and of Christ in all Scripture) are so instinctively. Ask them what their formula is and you will draw a blank expression. The principles they use have been developed unconsciously, through a combination of native ability, gift and experience as listeners and preachers. Some might struggle to give a series of lectures on how they go about preaching. Why? Because what they have developed is an *instinct*; preaching biblically has become their native language. They are able to use the grammar of biblical theology without reflecting on what part of speech they are using. That is why the best preachers are not necessarily the best instructors in homiletics, although they are, surely, the greatest inspirers of true preaching.

Most of us probably develop the instinct for biblical-theological and redemptive-historical preaching by the osmosis involved in listening to those who do it well. It is always wise to listen to such preachers and their preaching as though we had two minds – one through which the preaching of the word nourishes us, the other through which, simultaneously or on later reflection, asks: 'Why did this exposition nourish me in that way? What dynamics and principles were operative?' Seeing how the hidden principles work out in practice is the best way to make those principles our own so that they become the grammar of our preaching.

Christ is the prism where all light converges

Given that we are not to become 'method' preachers applying a programmatic formula for biblical preaching, there are nevertheless very important principles that help us to develop Christ-centred expository skills. As we work with them, and as they percolate through our thinking and our approach to the Bible, they will help us develop the instinct to point people to Christ from the Old Testament Scriptures.

The most general principle is one for which we might coin the expression *fillfulment*: Christ fulfils or 'fills full' the Old Testament. He came 'not to abolish the Law or the Prophets but to fulfil them' (Mt. 5:17). As Christians standing within the light of New Testament revelation and looking back on the Old Testament, Christ himself acts as a hermeneutical prism. Looking back through him, we see the white light of the unity of the truth of Jesus Christ broken down into its constituent colours in the pages of the Old Testament. Then, looking forwards, we see how the multi-coloured strands of Old Testament revelation converge in him. When we appreciate this we begin to see how the constituent colours unite in Christ and are related both to each other and to him. In this way we see how the Old Testament points forward to him. We see how sometimes one 'colour', sometimes another, or perhaps a combination of them, points forward to Jesus Christ, is related to Jesus Christ, and is fulfilled by Jesus Christ.

Principles for preaching Christ from the Old Testament

We want to develop an instinct to preach Christ. This is the general principle, but it can be broken down into at least four subordinate principles.

Principle 1. The relationship between promise and fulfilment

Genesis 3:15 is in a sense the most basic text in the whole Bible: God puts enmity between the seed of the serpent and the seed of the woman; the seed of the woman will bruise the head of the serpent, and the serpent will crush the heel of the woman's seed. Romans 16:20 and Revelation 12:9 both make crystal clear from the perspective of Christ's completed work that Genesis 3:15 promises the ultimate cosmic conflict between our Lord Jesus Christ and Satan and the powers of darkness.

Of course, Satan is not mentioned by name in Genesis 3 – a point of some hermeneutical interest in itself – but when Paul writes that 'the God of peace will bruise Satan under your head shortly' (Rom. 16:20), and John sees in Revelation 12:9 that the serpent has grown into a dragon, it is clear that the New Testament writers thought of Genesis 3:15 as a reference to the coming Messiah, and to his conflict with Satan. The war about which the book of Revelation speaks then merely climaxes an antithesis and antagonism that has run through the whole of Scripture. It is a Library of Military History, with Genesis 3:15 and Revelation 12:9 – 20:10 as the bookcase. Not only so, but it follows that the whole of Old Testament Scriptures traces the outworking of this promise of God until it is consummated in Jesus Christ, and finally publicized throughout the universe in his triumphant return. Jesus' programmatic statement, 'I will build my church, and the gates of Hades [hell] will not overcome it' (Mt. 16:18) speaks of this cosmic-conflict context, represents its high point and promises victory in it. Everything between Genesis 3:15 and Matthew

16:18 can, in one way or another, be tied to the fulfilment of that promise; every twist and turn in redemptive history following Matthew 16:18 expresses that conflict, flows onward to its denouement and to that extent can be pinpointed on the map of redemptive revelation.

This is the story of the building of the kingdom of God in all its various stages, over against the kingdom of this world. The promise that the kingdom/reign of God/heaven will come/is near/has arrived is therefore a structural key to redemptive history. From Genesis 3:15 to the end, the Bible is the story of God the Warrior coming to the aid of his people in order to deliver them from the kingdom of darkness and to establish his reign among, in and through them. This is what gives weight to the words of John the Baptist that 'the kingdom of heaven is near' (Mt. 3:2). Breaking the prophetic silence of the centuries, his message was of God's impending eschatological war-triumph. Judgment-wrath represented by the judgment axe was, for John, the inevitable implication on the dark side; forgiveness and the reign and kingdom-blessing of God was the good news for all who repented.

This kingdom-conflict-conquest-victory theme can be traced in all kinds of narrative perspectives and dimensions of Old Testament revelation. The central point is to see the Old Testament as intimately (although of course not exclusively) connected to this fundamental idea that there is a radical antithesis driving through the whole of redemptive history, between the building of the kingdom of God by his king, and the efforts of the powers of darkness to destroy that kingdom. Recognize this and much of Old Testament Scripture can readily be understood in terms of its position in the central nervous system of the Old Testament. It should be possible to move from all of these different points to this backbone promise that runs through the Old Testament Scripture to Jesus Christ.

This is an essential hermeneutical tool with which to relate historical developments in the Old Testament back to the promise of God and forward to the coming of Christ. At the same time we are able to treat these incidents (and the people involved in them) as real in their own right. For one of the dangers inherent in biblical-theological preaching is to minimize historical actuality in our anxiety to preach Christocentrically. The result can be as damaging to the integrity of our handling of the text as was patristic allegorizing. Sensitivity to the war in the heavenly realms being played out in history enables us to expound the concrete-historical and individual experiences of God's people, yet simultaneously to interpret and place them within the big picture, the meta-narrative of the whole Bible. The historical is thus taken seriously for its own sake, while at the same time it is preached as part of the story of the all-conquering Christ.

This – it needs to be underlined – is not the only principle to be employed. But it does not require great imagination to see how events in Old Testament history illustrate it: the narrative of Adam and Eve against the serpent, the story of Cain and Abel, of the City of God and the Tower of Babel, Israel and Egypt, David and Goliath. The book of Job is simply a dramatic microcosm of this. The conflicts and the miracles of Elijah and Elisha need to be read within this perspective. A submerged axehead or a poisoned stew are trivial problems, the miraculous reduced to a Harry Potter piece of magic, unless we recognize that these events take place in the context of a deadly conflict with eternal significance for the kingdom of God. Daniel's life story and his apocalyptic visions are to be read through the same lenses. Indeed, the opening words of the book of Daniel indicate that we are entering a conflict narrative. There is war between two kingdoms. Here we have both the onslaught of the powers of darkness and this world ('Nebuchadnezzar king of Babylon came to Jerusalem and besieged it') and the righteous purposes of God through which his kingdom will continue and prevail ('the Lord delivered Jehoiakim king of Judah into his hand . . .'). Under fierce attack it requires extraordinary miracles to preserve the kingdom (now a remnant of four, exposed to destroying fire and the mouths of lions, Daniel 3 and 6). In the midst of this the kingdom (and king!) of this world is seen to be temporary, and it and we are given intimation that it is the rock cut without human hands that will grow and fill the whole earth. Only those who see history this way (Daniel and his three friends) can sing the Lord's song in a foreign land, in enemy-occupied territory (Ps. 137).

In a similar way the opposition to the rebuilding of Jerusalem in the days of Ezra and Nehemiah is part of the unfolding of Genesis 3:15. These books provide conflict narratives in the confined space of God's chosen city, illustrating that the exhortations of Ephesians 6:10–20 are as relevant in fifth century BC Jerusalem as in first century AD Ephesus.

We stand on the other side of the empty tomb; what was 'not yet' for Ezra and Nehemiah is 'already' for us. But there is also a 'not yet' for us; the conflict in the mopping up operations of war is as bloody and potentially fatal as in the decisive battle. We too, in the light of what Christ has accomplished, live in the 'not yet-ness' of the completion of the final Jerusalem. This world is as full of the Tobiah, Sanballat and Geshem of Nehemiah's day as it is of the Mr Talkative and the Giant Despair and Vanity Fair of John Bunyan's *Pilgrim's Progress*.

Understanding the principle of promise and fulfilment in terms of an ongoing kingdom-against-kingdom cosmic-conflict helps us to apply the message of the Old Testament as Christian preachers today.

Principle 2. The relationship between type and antitype
As the principle of promise and fulfilment (in Christ) develops, we see how the rest of redemptive history functions as a kind of footnote to Genesis 3:15.

However, we also discover that the promise itself is developed both progressively and cumulatively; its implications become clearer as redemptive history unfolds. At particular stages in history God gives hints of what is to come (as a great artist's sketches point towards the final work). So embedded into redemptive history are illustrations of the pattern of working which God will employ in his masterwork – types that will be fulfilled in the work of Christ the antitype. Paul views the relation between Adam and Christ as the supreme illustration of this patterning; Adam, viewed as a real historical figure, is the *tupos* of the coming one (Rom. 5:14), albeit the analogy is both positive and negative (Rom. 5:12–21).

The Mosaic ceremonial and sacrificial system functions similarly, a prominent theme in the theology of the author of Hebrews. There is a real priesthood, real sacrifice and real blood. But these, while real, also signify a greater reality that accomplishes what they can only portray. Hebrews suggests that a genuine Old Testament believer, with the stench of the sacrificial blood clogging his nostrils, could deduce from the fact that the priests ministered in this way day after day that these could not be the sacrifices that bring forgiveness. He must look beyond this (and was able to), to that of which these sacrifices were a type – namely to God's covenant promises yet to be fulfilled, and therefore (as Hebrews makes so clear), to Jesus Christ himself.

But this principle of type and antitype operates in another, less technical sense, in what we could call the divine patterning of redemptive history. When we put 'the Christ event' under the microscope we see that there are basic patterns expressed which are first seen in the Old Testament. In the light of that discovery, when we re-read the Old Testament wearing the lenses of the New, we see these Christ-patterns more opaquely. The divine footprints are already visible.

An interesting illustration of this is the use of Hosea 11:1 in Matthew 2:15: 'Out of Egypt I called my son.' These words, Matthew says, are fulfilled in Christ. But isn't this either an esoteric or naïve approach to reading the Bible? Hosea is talking about the historic event of the people of God coming out of Egypt in the Exodus, not about Jesus going to and returning from Egypt in his infancy. So what is going on in Matthew's mind? Is he saying Hosea 11:1 is fulfilled in Jesus just as Isaiah 53 is? Yes. But not in the same sense.

Rather Matthew, writing in the light of the incarnation, death and resurrection of Jesus Christ, and under the guidance of the Holy Spirit, recognizes that the divine pattern in the Exodus (delivered from Egypt, led through the wilderness, given the covenant bond and kingdom-code) constitutes a *pattern* to be used in the experience of the true Israelite, Jesus Christ. In doing this Matthew provides us with a key to reading and expounding the entire Exodus narrative in a Christocentric way, and indeed his own narrative against a background that enriches our understanding of Jesus' identity and ministry.

Another example of this kind of pattern-repetition in redemptive history is that of Elisha healing the son of the Shunammite woman (2 Ki. 4:8–37). The miracles worked through Elisha demonstrate God's intimate care for ordinary people – the humble poor, the widow and the barren woman. The healing of the Shunammite's son echoes later in the town of Nain, where Jesus too healed a widow's son (Lk. 7:11–17). Luke surely means his readers to empathize with the mindset of the people in Nain who knew well that it was in their little community that the miracle had been accomplished through Elisha (who followed Elijah, the one whose return was promised, Mal. 4:5 and fulfilled in John the Baptist, Mt. 11:14). Nain was near the site of Old Testament Shunem. Even the reaction of the people of Nain to Jesus echoes with allusions to this distant event: 'A great prophet has appeared among us. God has come to help his people.' It is as if they are saying 'Something like this happened here before; and ever since Elisha, we have been looking forward to something even better still to come – *the* prophet himself. Could this be he?'

So we are meant to see pattern-repetition, which comes to its fullness in the person of Jesus Christ, the great prophet who heals not merely through delegated authority from God, but on his own authority, without rituals or prayers, but with a simple word of power. Here is the great God and Saviour of Israel in the flesh, whose person is both the origin and consummation of all the patterns and echoes which have prophesied this grace to his people all down the long ages of their history. Yes, God *has* visited his people, at last, in the person of his Son. But clearly this sheds light backwards on the function of Elisha. Now we see the significance of his healing within both the micro-reality of his personal context, and also within the macro-reality of his significance in the patterns of redemptive history.

As we work intimately with the two Testaments, we will increasingly recognize the echoes of the Old Testament. And as we become sensitive to these patterns and allusions, lines from the Old Testament to Christ will become clearer to us and easier to draw.[3]

Principle 3. The relationship between the covenant and Christ

In the New Testament Jesus himself embodies all that the covenant signified in the Old Testament. His is the blood of the new covenant (Lk. 22:20). He fulfils all the covenant promises of God. 'For no matter how many promises God has made, they are "Yes" in Christ' (2 Cor. 1:20).

The covenant promises of God form the scaffolding that God was putting in place as he directed redemptive history towards the coming of Jesus Christ. The scaffolding in the Old Testament is therefore built around the person and work of our Lord Jesus Christ and shaped by him. We can see this in two ways.

First, there is the principle that in the covenant relationship the imperatives of God (his laws and commands) are always rooted in the indicatives of his grace. That is how the covenant works: 'I will be your God; you will be my people.' This is scaffolding shaped around Christ and the gospel. For this is how the gospel works: 'I will die for you; therefore trust in and obey me.' The dynamic of the Old Testament covenant was shaped with a view to the coming of Jesus Christ.

We can go further to say this: that which was promised by God in the Covenant at Sinai, and demanded by God in terms of its imperatives, did not have a sufficiently strong foundation to effect what it commanded. Geographical relocation is not an adequate support to provide the dynamic for Decalogue-style moral holiness (*cf.* Rom. 8:3–4). A geographical resettlement may motivate, but it cannot cancel the guilt of sin or empower morally. Thus the Sinai covenant – in its weakness – was always prophetic of a greater and fuller deliverance through God's redeeming grace. '*I* am the LORD your God who brought you out of the land of *Egypt* . . . You shall have no other gods before me' (Ex. 20:2–3, my emphasis) was always a statement that looked forwards as well as backwards. Written into the way in which the old covenant works is an implied expectation, even necessity, that the indicatives of God's grace will find a better consummation and the imperatives a better foundation – in Jesus Christ.

Secondly, the shape of Christ's work is expressed in the covenant principle of blessing and cursing.

Today our appreciation of much of the Bible's language has become very threadbare. There is a tendency to think that the words 'blessing' and 'cursing' function in a relatively trivial manner, equivalent to a kind of divine 'boo-hurrah' approach to morality. When someone sneezes, we say 'Bless you!' Few people set this within the historical context of the pre-modern world when sneezing was a symptom of the plague. It was therefore seen potentially as a sign of the displeasure of God. One prayed that the person sneezing would receive the blessing of God and *therefore not perish*. That is much nearer the Bible's understanding of blessing and cursing than our usage is.

Blessing is not 'Have a nice day!' nor is cursing 'You are a bit of a pain in the neck'. Rather, here is God's covenant; when we respond to it in faith, he showers upon us the blessing he promised when he made it with us. And when we respond in unbelief, he showers upon us curses (*cf.* Dt. 27 – 30). The gospel is that Christ took the curse of the covenant in order that the blessings of the covenant (promised to Abraham) might come to us (Gal. 3:13). Paul's thinking here is both redemptive-historical and biblical-theological. He recognizes that all of this covenantal outworking of blessing and cursing in the Old Testament is inextricably tied to the fulfilment of God's covenant purpose and promise in Jesus Christ.

This principle of Christ as the heart of the covenants of God, with respect to their blessing and cursing, helps us expound and apply the Old Testament as a covenant-focused message in the light of the fulfilment of both blessing and cursing in Christ. The consequences bound up in the covenant blessing and cursing point us forwards inexorably, if typologically, to the eternal consequences of acceptance or rejection of the gospel. The contents of biblical history and wisdom literature, prophecy and the psalms all reveal this covenant dynamic. Insofar as this is true, we are able to relate them to the ultimate fulfilment of that dynamic in Christ and the gospel.

Principle 4. Proleptic participation and subsequent realization

Despite the continuing influence within evangelicalism of various brands of dispensationalism, it lies on the surface of the apostolic writings that the majority of illustrations of salvation in the new covenant era are actually drawn from the old! Of course the apostles recognize the substantial discontinuity between old and new. Pentecost is indeed a quantum leap forward. But that notwithstanding, when Paul wants to illustrate how the gospel works, he goes back to the Old Testament figures of Abraham and David and says '*This* is how the gospel works.' A seismic shift took place after Pentecost so that the least in the kingdom is greater than the greatest of the prophets (John the Baptist, Mt. 11:11). Men and women of faith do not come to perfection apart from new covenant believers who experience better things (Heb. 11:40). Nevertheless Abel, Enoch, Noah, Abraham, Isaac, Jacob, Joseph, Moses, Rahab, Gideon, Barak, Samson, Jephthah, David, Samuel and the prophets are examples of faith (Heb. 11). We receive salvation 'better', but not a better salvation. If you want to know what the Christian life looks like, then there is much to be learned from the Old Testament! What right-thinking Christian has not aspired to experience the whole-souled faith and worship of the Psalms?

But how could Old Testament believers experience grace and the fruit of the Spirit? They experienced *proleptic participation* in what would be consummated in Jesus Christ and then subsequently realized in its fulness in post-Pentecost Christian believers.

Orthodox evangelical Christians employ the principle of proleptic participation with respect to justification. Were Old Testament saints justified by grace, and if so, how? Yes, of course – by faith in the promise of the Saviour. We who are as far removed in time as Abraham was from Christ are justified because we believe in the once-promised Christ now come. But through the promise of God, Abraham experienced in proleptic fashion what we now experience in the light of the actuality of the incarnation.

But exactly the same principle operates in the area of sanctification – both definitive (the once-for-all separation from the dominion of sin which takes place in regeneration) and progressive (the ongoing overcoming of the presence and influence of sin which takes place throughout the Christian life). For justification and sanctification, while distinguishable, are not separable in either old or new covenant realities. Saints in the Old Testament were justified in the light of what Christ would do; they were sanctified in the same way: their lives were shaped and formed in the light of what Christ would do. An example of that is seen in Hebrews 10:39: 'We are not of those who shrink back and are destroyed, but of those who believe and who are saved.' But from what source does the author illustrate this principle of the grace of perseverance? From the Old Testament! Old Testament saints were commended for their faith, yet none of them had received what had been promised. God had planned something better for us and only together with us would they be made perfect. What they experienced then was a proleptic, anticipatory, form of the reality we better experience in its fullness, namely the working out of union and communion with Jesus Christ.

It is the perspective of the New Testament that from the moment an individual becomes a believer, his or her life is shaped providentially by God and pressed into a mould which takes its form from the dying and rising of Jesus, and is shaped by his crucifixion and resurrection, his death bringing new life. In sanctification God transforms us into the likeness of his Son, so that reminiscences of Jesus Christ crucified and resurrected appear in us, and the pattern of death and resurrection shapes our lives – these are the genuine biblical *stigmata* in which all believers share.

But this pattern is also present in the lives of Old Testament saints. Admittedly the fascination with typology in some evangelical groupings has been unfortunate and without controls; but nevertheless a Christ-shape and a Christ-pattern appear clearly in a variety of Old Testament saints, and must ultimately be analysed as a shadow in their lives created by the backwards projection into history of the work of Christ.

There are so many illustrations of this that one might almost say that there is not an Old Testament historical-biographical account of any length that does not involve dying and rising, humiliation and exaltation, being brought down and being raised up, experiencing opposition and then deliverance, suffering want and then experiencing extraordinary provision. This is not merely the form of good story-telling, it is the embodiment of the gospel pattern.

Joseph is a classic case: the story of his life is shaped unmistakably by the pattern of death and resurrection. A pattern is written large in him: humiliation (rejected and stripped of his glory-robe, becoming a slave, being made of no reputation)→ exaltation (being highly exalted at Pharaoh's right hand)→ provision (for the needs of the whole world)→ the ingathering of his people. This, at the end of the day, is the Christ-pattern in sketch-like form. The pattern of meant-for-evil→ producing good, the salvation of many (Gn. 50:20) is fulfilled in the one crucified by the hands of wicked men – yet according to the plan of the God who raised him from the dead for the salvation of the nations (Acts 2:23). That same pattern, while written large in Joseph, appears throughout the Old Testament. It connects the Old Testament saints to Christ, and underlines that we do not fully understand their experience apart from this template.

Developing a Christ-centred instinct

If these principles hold good, then it must be possible along different lines, sometimes using one, sometimes using a combination, to move from any point in the Old Testament into the backbone of redemptive history which leads ultimately to Christ its fulfilment and consummation. In this way, the context and destination for all our preaching will be Jesus Christ himself, Saviour and Lord.

These are general principles; they do not constitute a simple formula, an elixir to be sprinkled on our sermons to transform them into the preaching of Christ. There is no formula that will do that. We never 'arrive' or 'have it cracked' when it comes to preaching Christ. But as we come to know the Scriptures more intimately, as we see these patterns deeply embedded in the Bible, and – just as crucially – as we come to know Christ himself more intimately and to love him better, we shall surely develop the instinct to reason, explain and prove from all the Scriptures the riches of grace which are proclaimed in Jesus, the Christ, the Saviour of the world. The ability to do that will itself be adequate reward for the hard work involved in learning to preach in a way that takes the Old Testament seriously within its own context, but also recognizes that that context is not complete apart from Jesus Christ.

Notes

1. This is true despite the fact that the great Princeton scholar Geerhardus Vos was already appointed to teach biblical theology (in this sense of the discipline) in the last decade of the nineteenth century and gave his inaugural lecture on that subject in 1894; see R. B. Gaffin, Jr (ed.), *Redemptive History and Biblical Interpretation: The Shorter Writings of Geerhardus Vos* (Philipsburg, NJ: Presbyterian and Reformed, 1980), pp. x, 3–24.

2. 'The Biblical Doctrine of the Trinity' in *The Works of B. B. Warfield*, vol. 2, *Biblical Doctrines* (New York: Oxford University Press, 1929), pp. 141–142.

3. A useful manual in this context is the 'Index of Allusions and Verbal Parallels' printed in the corrected 3rd edition of *The Greek New Testament* (United Bible Societies, 1983), ed. K. Aland, et. al., pp. 901–911.

II

6

The preacher as theologian

Preaching and systematic theology

J. I. Packer

It is widely imagined that one can fulfil the preacher's role without being a theologian. This thought is of a piece with the idea that one can fulfil the theologian's role without being a preacher. I should like to assault both notions together, for both are perverse; but you cannot kick with two feet simultaneously, and in any case the title to which I have been asked to write limits me to countering the first. So here I aim simply to show how needful it is for a preacher to be a theologian. To this end I shall reflect first on the nature of theology, second on the nature of preaching, and third on the vital value of theological awareness and competence for the performing of the preacher's task.

Theology

At the start of each academic year at Regent College all professors are asked to strut a few minutes of their stuff for the orientation of incoming students. I regularly begin my bit of the programme by declaring myself to be a servant of the Queen – that is, of theology, the true queen of the sciences; and then I give a sort of Identikit profile of the lady who commands my allegiance. I refer to her *sight*, explaining that she has to wear glasses, since she can see nothing clearly till she looks at it through the lens of Holy Scripture. I speak of her *shape*, indicating that she has a graceful – that is, a grace-full – figure, which she works to keep by devotional and doxological habits of God-centred thinking. And I say that she is *sassy* – which is American for *saucy*, and signifies a perkiness that Americans admire (not as it was in the England of Dick Lucas' and my youth, where *sauce* meant *cheek*, and 'None of your sauce!' was an ultimate put-down). I define the sassiness of theology as an unwillingness to keep quiet when God is misrepresented and revealed truth is put in jeopardy. Then I urge that these character qualities should appear in all the Queen's servants, particularly those who plan to preach.

Pursuing the picture, we may truly say that though the Queen is not always properly clad in public, when she is she is most impressive. Truth, wisdom, devotion, breadth, clarity and practicality are then the leading motifs of her ensemble, and the ensemble itself consists of ten linked disciplines. The first is *exegesis*, for which the question always is: what was this or that biblical text written to convey to its readers?[1] The second is *biblical theology*, for which the question is: what is the total message of the canonical books on this or that subject? The third is *historical theology*, the bonding glue of church history, exploring how Christians in the past viewed specific biblical truths. The fourth is *systematic theology*, which rethinks biblical theology with the help of historical theology in order to restate the faith, topic by topic and as a whole, in relation to current interests, assumptions, questions, hopes, fears and uncertainties in today's church and world. The fifth is *apologetics*, which seeks to commend and defend the faith as rational and true in face of current unbelief, misbelief and puzzlement. The sixth is *ethics*, which systematizes the standards of Christian life and conduct and applies them to particular cases. The seventh is *spiritual theology*, sometimes called devotional or ascetic theology or Christian spirituality, which studies how to understand and maintain sanctifying communion with God. The eighth is *missiology*, which aims to see how God's people should view and tackle their gospel-spreading, church-planting and welfare-bringing tasks across cultural barriers world-wide. The ninth is *liturgy*, which asks how God is best and most truly worshipped, and how true worship may be achieved in existing churches. The tenth is *practical theology*, embracing pastoral theology, family theology and political theology as it explores how to further God's work and glory in home, church and society.

Full-dressed as distinct from half-dressed theology, if I may put it so, will show competence in all these disciplines. Theology is often described as a quadrilateral of biblical, historical, theological and practical studies, but the ten-discipline analysis is more precise.[2] Theological education latches on to it, and constructs its syllabi accordingly.

The focus of the Queen's outfit is systematic theology, which draws its raw material from the first three disciplines and serves the church by providing resources of digested truth for the last six. It is called *systematic* not because it works by speculative inferences about God, or by scaling him down so as to dissolve away the mystery of his being and render him manageable by our minds (both those procedures would falsify his reality), but because it takes all the truths, visions, valuations and admonitions with which the Holy Spirit feeds the church through the Scriptures and seeks to think them together in a clear, coherent and orderly way. It separates out seven main topical fields – revelation; God; man; Christ; the Holy Spirit; the church; the future[3] – and fills in all that Scripture is found to say about each. In the past this discipline was called *dogmatic theology* and given the task of analysing, crystallizing and where necessary recasting those biblical truths that the church has committed itself to uphold and teach. The description derives not from dogmatism and rigidity as a personal style among theologians (perish the thought!) but from *dogma*, a Greek word meaning that which has been decided. *Systematic*, however, seems to me the better label, both because integrated spelling out of revealed truth as such is the goal and because everything taught in the Bible is theology's business, whether or not the church's creeds include it.

Systematic theology moves between, and regularly blends, three styles of thought and speech, each of which needs separate appreciation for the job it does. These are the *kerygmatic*, exploring in comprehensive terms the question 'What is the Bible telling us?'; the *confessional*, exploring in contemporary terms, with all sorts of interactions, the question 'How should the church assert this so as to be heard?'; and the *philosophical*, exploring in logical terms the question 'What is the exact meaning of these biblical and churchly affirmations?' For success in the first mode, listening to the Bible is all-important; for success in the second mode, listening to the world is what matters; for success in the third mode, listening to the technicians of language and communication is what counts. Still pursuing our parable, we could describe these three styles as the three-tone colour scheme of the Queen's dress. We should note that theology's technical terms mostly belong to styles two and three, where their role is to highlight the gems displayed in essentially biblical language by style one.

The fact that systematic theology provides the raw material for disciplines five through to ten as listed above shows clearly enough that systematic theology is to the church's health as diet is to the body's health: health suffers if what is ingested is not right. All aspects of practical Christianity will be weakened if 'systematics' is neglected. Christian history has seen many movements of experience-oriented reaction against theology's supposedly barren intellectualism. These movements have thought they could get on without serious theological study, and have discouraged their adherents from engaging in it. In the short term, while living on theological capital brought in from outside by their founders, they have often channelled spiritual life in an impressive way, but with the passage of time they have again and again lapsed into old errors and forms of imbalance and stuntedness which, for lack of theological resources, they are unable effectively to correct, and which prompt the rest of the church to stand back from them. 'No-one ever tried to break logic but what logic broke him' is a dictum ascribed to A. S. Pringle-Pattison;[4] something similar has to be said about systematic theology.

The above portrayal of the Queen of the sciences is, of course, ideal. In practice, systematic theologians often fall short through overlooking or disregarding biblical data, or handling it in terms of some distorting paradigm of understanding or of truth that is abroad in either the church or the world or both. There are only three methods of procedure, fundamentally speaking, in theological work; the one we have surveyed, which I call *biblicist*; that which appeals to supposedly infallible pronouncements by the church as the ultimate standard, a method which I call *traditionalist*; and the procedure which, having reviewed the deliverances of Scripture and the history of Christian thought by the light of contemporary secular opinions, treats the dictates of the theologian's reason, conscience, or immediate religious awareness as God's truth for that time, a method which I call *subjectivist*. No-one can study theology without coming to regard two of those three as radically wrong; but any of them can be adulterated by inconsistent slidings from time to time at the level of method. So, with God's help, self-assessment (in terms of our bit of whimsy, the Queen examining herself in the mirror of Holy Scripture) and self-reformation (the Queen tidying herself as the mirror shows she needs to do) are regularly required of those who, correctly, follow the biblicist method as best they can. I say 'as best they can' because we should not expect ever in this world to reach a point where the church and the Christian have nothing more to set straight or to take in at convictional level: such perfection is for heaven, and is not given here.

But here and now we all need the best theology we can get. Every time we mention God we become theologians, and the only question is whether we are going to be good ones or bad ones. And this touches both thought and life. Older writers affirmed, and our ten-discipline analysis showed, that theology is a 'theoretico-practical' study – 'the science of living blessedly for ever', as William Perkins, the Puritan, breathtakingly defined it.[5] As a critical and analytical exploration of the evidence of revelation about reality (God, and life under God), and as a developed intellectual organism interpreting and prescribing for the human condition according to its own insight into reality, theology may well be called a science, with a life enriched by God as its end-product. It moves to that end-product in two stages.

First, it leads to a deeper understanding of the Bible, by giving us an ordered overview of what is demonstrably in the Bible and so telling us what to look for in the Bible. When my wife and I walk in the country, she sees far more than I do, not because her eyes work better than mine, but because she is a naturalist who recognizes birds, trees, plants, little animals, and much more when she sees them. I, by contrast, see without understanding – without observing, as Sherlock Holmes expressed it in his criticism of Dr Watson. To be sure, the boot is on the other foot when we inspect old-fashioned steam railway loco-motives: all my wife knows is that they are water-boilers on wheels, self-propelled; but I, who once hoped to be an engine-driver, know more about them than that, and consequently see more of what I am looking at than she does. The point is that prior theoretical knowledge enables you to observe more of what is there. In Bible study, the theologically unaware are likely to overlook the significance of what they read; which is why Calvin tailored the second and subsequent editions of his *Institutes* as a preparation for exploring the Scriptures themselves.[6] In this he may have shown more wisdom than do some of the theorists of what is called nowadays 'inductive Bible study', who tell you to 'observe' without giving you any theological orientation to help you do it.

Since the Reformation the cardinal principle of biblical interpretation among Protestants has been *Sacra Scriptura sui ipsius interpres* – the Holy Scripture is its own interpreter, interpreting itself. The assumption is that proper interpretation will bring out a rational coherence and consistency that are already there in the text, since it all comes from a single divine mind, and God the Holy Spirit can be trusted not to have contradicted himself in masterminding the writing of the sixty-six books. The assumption is valid and the method is right, but we shall still get along far faster if we have available a catechetical-level theology, that is, a crystallized and digested overview of biblical teaching as a whole, with the main emphases brought out, that will help us to see what we are looking at in each biblical passage. Especially is this so with regard to biblical statements about God, where each noun, adjective and verb that is used of God – that is, that God, the primary author of the text, uses of himself – bears a sense that at points differs from its sense when used of humans. The appropriate adjustment for us to make in each case is to drop the associations of finitude and moral limitation that all words used of humans naturally carry, and replace them with notions of the infinite self-existence and moral glory that some texts ascribe to God explicitly. Inductive Bible study would doubtless make one aware of the need for this adjustment as one kept comparing Scripture with Scripture over the years, but to have theology make it explicit and drill one in it from the start advances one's understanding more quickly. From this standpoint, to speak of theology as the science of Bible study is both true and illuminating.

Second, theology teaches us how to apply revealed truth for the leading of our lives; thus theology guides our steps, grants us vision, and fuels our worship, while at the same time disinfecting our minds from the inadequate, distorted and corrupt ideas of God and godliness that come naturally to our fallen intellect. These ideas, if not correct, will mislead us and hold us back, and perhaps totally derail us, in our Christian practice, and will certainly be a stumbling-block to those whom we seek to help. Before you can become a physician or a garage mechanic you need a thorough theoretical grounding, in the one case in physiology and pathology, in the other in the mechanisms and mainten-ance of cars, and without it you would inevitably do damage – perhaps a great deal of damage. Similarly, we need a proper theoretical grounding in the life of faith and obedience before we can either live that life consistently ourselves or help anyone else to do so. Guided by theology, however, we may start to experience 'living blessedly for ever' in peace, hope, joy and love Godward, and be able to help others into that same supernaturalized existence.

These enrichments to which theology leads are crucial for all Christians, but particularly for preachers, as we shall see.

Preaching

A theological account of theology, formally viewed, is now before us. In this section a similar account of preaching will be set beside it.

What is preaching? Sociologically and institutionally, preaching has to be defined in terms of pulpits and pews, meetings and programmes, and corporate expectations fulfilled more or less by the monologue of a stated leader. Our biblical and theological approach, however, leads to a definition in terms of divine purpose rather than human performance. The definition comes out thus: preaching is incarnational communica-tion from God, prophetic, persuasive and powerful – that is, power-full. Let me explain.

First, preaching is *communication*. God, our Maker and Redeemer, is constantly speaking his word to the human race, and within it particularly to his own believing people. That word is his message of grace to sinners, which he spoke definitively in and through the Christ-centred revelatory and redemptive process that the Bible records, and now speaks definitively in and through the biblical record itself. God makes himself known by telling us specific things about himself and about ourselves in relation to him, and thus he invites and draws us into repentance, faith, love, and new life in restored friendly fellowship with himself. The text of the Bible, which from this standpoint may properly be described as God preaching to us, is the primary form of this communication, and the messages of preachers who faithfully relay the elements of God's total message constitute its derivative form. Jesus Christ, the Son of God incarnate, crucified, risen, ascended, reigning and returning, is the focal centre of God's communication; the new-covenant relationship between God and ourselves through Christ is its immediate announced objective; and the sanctifying of all life under Christ to the glory of God and the blessing of mankind is its ultimate goal. Preachers are only preachers, that is, messengers of God, so far as they understand these things, keep them in sight, and make them the staple substance of their own messages. Pulpiteers who deliver anything different or anything less are failing to communicate God's message, and that means they are not preachers in the theological sense of that word.

Second, preaching is *prophetic* communication. The prophets of Bible times functioned as God's spokesmen and sounding-boards. They passed on oracular and visionary messages, admonitory, hortatory and revelatory, which God had given them; they were not sources, but channels. The Christian preacher must function in the same way. To be sure, he will do it in a didactic mode, like the apostles, who spoke as God-taught teachers, rather than in the dualistic mode of the prophets, whose ministry of instruction was limited to faithfulness as God's messenger-boys whom he could trust to deliver his oracles word for word. But in making it his business to confront people not with his own ideas, as such, but with the contents of the Word of God, the Christian preacher will show himself to stand in the prophetic succession. The words of the man who preaches must carry the word of the God who speaks.

It thus appears that all true preaching is biblical interpretation – that is, elucidation and application of 'God's Word written'.[7] Preaching means speaking God's own message in his name, that is, as his representative; and this is possible for us, with our sin-twisted minds, only as we labour faithfully to echo, re-state and re-apply God's once-for-all witness to himself in Holy Scripture. Biblical interpretation means theological exegesis of the text, in relation to the rest of the organism of revealed truth, for the scripturally defined purposes of teaching, reproof, correction and training in righteousness (*cf.* 2 Tim.

3:16–17). Such applicatory interpretation chimes in with the nature and purpose of all the canonical books as their human authors conceived them, and is in fact the most faithful and right-minded handling of them that can be imagined. It is worth pausing to illustrate this.

In their character as God's mouthpieces the prophets proclaimed, and then wrote down, messages that were essentially God's appeals to Israel for repentance, righteousness, fidelity and true worship. Christians' hearts are to be searched by them, just as were the hearts of Old Testament saints and sinners, and true preachers will apply them so.

In their role as Christ's commissioned agents and ambassadors (cf. 2 Cor. 5:20), the apostles wrote letters of exhortation and direction – epistolary sermons – to keep Christians on track. God means them to do that job for us today, and true preachers will use them accordingly.

The Old Testament historians, whom the Jews perceptively called the former prophets, told of God's dealings with people and nations in a way that was clearly meant to evoke praise and teach lessons about faith and obedience on the one hand, and unbelief and disobedience on the other. These lessons were meant to mould and shape readers' lives for God, and true preachers today will enforce them to that end.

The gospels prove on inspection to be not artless memoirs of Jesus, (as was once thought) but four careful selections of stories about his sayings, doings, and sufferings, all so arranged and angled that 'the gospel' – the life-changing news of a divine Saviour – will leap out into the thoughtful reader's mind and heart. True preachers will bring this out, and spend their strength to make it happen.

The wisdom books (of which it was well said[8] that the Psalms teach us how to praise, the Proverbs how to live, the Song of Solomon how to love, Job how to endure, and Ecclesiastes how to enjoy) are didactic preaching in substance, and should be expounded accordingly.

So we might go on. When Paul said that 'everything that was written in the past was written to teach us, so that through . . . the encouragement of the Scriptures we might have hope' (Rom. 15:4), his thought was that God meant all the Old Testament books to function in due course as his own preaching to Christians. So the Bible itself must preach, and must be seen and felt to preach, in all our preaching. The Westminster Directory for Public Worship was right to require preachers, when raising a point from a text, to labour to let their hearers see 'how God teaches it from thence'[9] – in other words, to show that it is being read out of the sacred text, not read into it. This is the true prophetic dimension of preaching.[10]

Third, preaching is *persuasive* communication. Persuasion in a good cause expresses both respect for others as rational beings and concern for their welfare, as persons not yet fully abreast of the way of truth and wisdom. Persuasion was how Paul defined his evangelistic ministry ('we try to persuade . . . we implore . . . we urge'; 2 Cor. 5:11, 20; 6:1), and persuasion was how Luke described it (Acts 18:4; 19:8; 28:23). Though the Bible is clear that hearts are changed, and faith and faithfulness generated, only by the new-creating power of God, it is equally clear that persuasion is the means we are meant to use if changed lives are what we want to see. Christian persuasion is a matter of giving reasons, factual and prudential, for embracing the belief and behaviour that constitute discipleship to Jesus Christ, and then of pressing God's commands, promises, warnings and assurances, with a view to winning one's hearer or hearers (or, if it is being done by writing, one's readers) to a positive response. Preaching is not bludgeoning and browbeating, but persuading. This is its only proper style, the path of patent and patient love.

Fourth, preaching is *power-full* communication. The reference here is not to loud shouting, pulpit-beating for emphasis, or any other display of animal energy, but to the way God is pleased to link the ministry of the Holy Spirit with the ministry of the Word, so that the preached message pierces hearers' hearts. Paul speaks of this when he says that at Corinth, where people expected him as a travelling pundit to show off his learning, and where he had resolved to stick to 'the testimony about God . . . Jesus Christ and him crucified', 'my message and my preaching were not with wise and persuasive words [he is being ironic, and means 'frivolously captivating'; he is not contradicting 2 Cor. 5:11!], but with a demonstration of the Spirit's power, so that your faith might not rest on men's wisdom, but on God's power' (1 Cor. 2:1–5). The assumption reflected here is that, other things being equal, the Holy Spirit will give the preacher a gift of understanding and utterance that will cause the word spoken to make a spiritual impact and bring forth spiritual fruits. In experience, other things are not always equal. The preacher's message, heart, life, and approach to the particular preaching situation may be insufficiently Christ-centred and bad in a number of ways. He may fail to be clear, or to commend himself credibly as a serious and humble servant of Jesus Christ. He may have grown proudly self-reliant, and neglected to pray for his preaching. If he comes across as a mechanical formalist whose heart is not in his communicating, or as a self-absorbed, manipulative, and untrustworthy person, or as a play-actor indulging in unreality with his pulpit dramatics and rhetoric, no spiritual impact is likely. Factors in the hearers as well as in the speaker may also quench the Spirit. But where the Spirit is unquenched the power of God will be present to work with and through the Word, and an impact will be made for God.

Fifth, preaching is *incarnational* communication. Phillips Brooks indicated this when he declared that preaching is truth through personality, though 'personhood', I think, would express his thought

more precisely. The point is that the preacher is inescapably part of the
message. He must model by his demeanour both the authority of the
truths he is communicating and the response to them that he seeks to
evoke. There is no substitute for this: spiritual reality in the sense
defined is a 'must'. Preachers should seek it, but only their hearers will
know if they have found it. Without it, however, preaching in the
theological sense does not occur, and so the speaker's post-sermon
question, 'Did I *preach*?', becomes a necessary enquiry.

Preacher and theologian

Having seen, at least in formal theological outline, what theology and
preaching essentially are, we can now develop the point towards which
we have been driving from the start, namely that a preacher needs to be
a theologian of some competence in order to do his job.

I make here a number of assumptions. The first is that the preacher
is a congregational leader, recognized as such, to whom people look as
an embodiment of true Christianity, and whose preaching is heard as
setting standards for himself and his hearers alike. The second is that
his role makes him the principal agent in the theological and spiritual
formation of those to whom he regularly preaches, and that he is
answerable to God for the strategy of teaching and application that he
pursues as a means to that end. The third is that teaching with
application – preaching, that is – in a worship context is the main
means of a congregation's spiritual formation, whatever other occasions
and modes of instruction may be programmed into its life. The fourth
is that the anti-intellectual thrust of pietisms in the church and
relativisms in the world has left late-twentieth-century congregations,
and the Christians who make them up, much less concerned about
doctrinal truth than they need to be, so that a conscience about and an
appetite for learning the Word of God has to be created. The fifth is
that all members of all modern western congregations are constantly
confronted by deviant opinions and value systems, such as the anti-
Christianity of Jehovah's Witnesses, Mormons, and the New Age, the
out-of-shape Christianity of Roman Catholicism, the watered-down,
indeed washed-out Christianity of Protestant liberalism, and the post-
Christian hedonism, materialism, and cynicism projected by the media,
the movies, and the books, plays, newspapers, magazines, schools,
universities, and politicians that combine to become opinion-makers for
tomorrow; and Christians have to be taught how to resist the
brainwashing impact of these aberrations. The present-day preacher
faces a formidable task of adult Christian education, and must plan his
pulpit strategy in a way that will teach discrimination in face of
deviation and fortitude in holding fast to truth. It will not suffice, in an

age like ours, for sermons to be isolated utterances, however noble each might be; they need to form a syllabus, covering the whole waterfront of challenges to revealed truth as well as the full landscape of the truth itself. Whether the sermons are announced in syllabus terms is not important; what matters is that the preacher should be facing up to his instructional and formational responsibility, and preaching according to his own thought-out strategy for discharging it.

My submission is that he cannot hope to meet this requirement completely unless he knows his way around in the fields of systematic theology, apologetics, ethics, and spiritual life. He needs to be well versed in the implications of a God-centred view of this created world and life within it. He needs to be deeply knowledgeable about the damage done to mankind's thought-life and moral nature by sin, the anti-God allergy in our fallen make-up that controls our pre-regenerate existence. He needs a thorough understanding of God's plan of salvation through Jesus Christ the mediator and of the regenerating work of the Holy Spirit in its intellectual, volitional, emotional and transformational aspects. He needs to be especially clear on what is involved in the authentic Christian life of faith, repentance, hope, love, self-denial, humility, dependence, and pleasing and worshipping and glorifying God; the life of faithful perseverance under pressure and of sustained spiritual warfare against the world, the flesh and the devil; the life of prayer to, and fellowship with, the Father and the Son; the life of sanctification and service, adoration and assurance, through the inward ministry of the Holy Spirit. He must know, and be able to show, what is involved, not only at the centre but also at the edges, in maintaining biblical standards, attitudes, and lifestyle distinctives in a world of competing religions and ideologies on the one hand and rampant irreligion and demoralization on the other. Amid all the cross-currents of our tempest-tossed culture he must be able to communicate in and through his expositions – that is, to let the Bible communicate through him – a sustained vision of consistent, triumphant, God-fearing and God-honouring Christian life. I venture to affirm that if he is not something of a theologian, permanently apprenticed to the ten disciplines listed earlier because he sees them as fundamental to the pastoral life, the task will prove to be far beyond him.

For, in the first place, only theology as described will secure for our preaching *adequacy of coverage*. All we who preach have our favourite themes on which we like to harp, and our areas of chronic neglect where, because our interest is less, we are tempted to leave the necessary thinking and teaching to somebody else. But the pastoral preacher's mandate, like Paul's, is 'to proclaim . . . the whole will [counsel, plan, purpose, intention, requirement] of God' (Acts 20:27). The substance and thrust of our sermons must come not only from personal vision and excitement about an old war-horse theme or a recent enthusiasm, plus our general sense of what might do some people some good, but from our focused knowledge of the range of revealed truth as well. We must know what are the fundamentals, the trunk and main branches of the Christian tree – the sovereignty of God in creation, providence, and grace; the trinitarian specifics of the Apostles' Creed; justification by faith alone through Christ's substitutionary atonement; salvation by grace alone through the regenerating work of the Holy Spirit; the centrality of the church in the Father's purposes; the coming return of Christ to judgment, and the certainty that heaven's glory or hell's misery will be everyone's final destiny. These fundamentals must be faithfully and thoroughly taught, just as the basic principles of our spiritual life at home, in the church and in the world must be. Countering mistaken notions as one goes along, and showing that Christianity is a faith that has reason on its side, are further elements in the preacher's task; how much of this is done on each occasion will depend on the text and the preacher's judgment of what the congregation needs, but though incidental it is very much part of the agenda. I should state explicitly that in saying these things I have in view not topical theological lectures in the pulpit – that, to my mind, could never be right – but rather biblical expository sermons, appropriately angled. Unless our preparation for regular preaching includes regular theological study, however, the above specifications are unlikely to be met. We who preach might well examine ourselves on this point before going further with the argument.

In the second place, only theology as described will secure *accuracy of exposition*. The story of the unskilled preacher who took the text, 'How shall we escape if we neglect such a great salvation?' (Heb. 2:3), and announced that his headings would be (1) the greatness of the salvation and (2) hints for escaping if we neglect it, has a warning for us here. Exposition must be accurate. Because the preacher shows what the text means for us today, and does not stop short of what it meant for its first readers, he rather than the academic commentator is the true interpreter of the Bible. But we reach the present-day meaning via the historical meaning, and while inductive exegesis of the text in its context is the finally authoritative method for achieving this, systematic theology, which is a digest of the findings of generations of Bible students, will constantly point us in the right direction. Donald Macleod thus comments on the description of Jesus Christ, God's Son, as 'the firstborn of all creation' (Col. 1:15, NRSV): 'All that the church learned in the Arian controversy forbids us to tolerate any exegesis that compromises either the pre-existence or the deity (creatorhood) of the Savior',[11] and he is right. To be sure, the references in the letter itself to all the fullness of God being in Christ (1:19; 2:9) confirm the wrongness of the Arian exegesis, which made the Son the first and noblest of the creatures, called 'Son' as an honorific courtesy title; but guidance in this matter from seventeen centuries of text-tested theology is not to be sneezed at.

Macleod gives a further example:

> . . . the notorious crux, Hebrews 6:4ff.: 'For it is impossible for those who were once enlightened and have tasted the heavenly gift and been made partakers of the Holy Spirit and have tasted the good word of God and the powers of the age to come, if they fall away, to renew them to repentance.' *Prima facie* this passage suggests that true believers can commit apostasy. Dogmatics alerts us, however, to the fact that such an interpretation is untenable, and closer examination of the passage itself confirms that it is pointing in the direction of another doctrine altogether – the doctrine of temporary faith.[12]

So we might go on, if there was need. As a guide in, and a check on, exegesis, theology can be invaluable.

There are areas of revealed truth that confront us starkly with the incomprehensible mystery of God's being and ways. In these areas the basic biblical conceptions are not always easy to hold on to, and it is easy to mishandle texts that embody them. If, for instance, we lack a biblical understanding of the Trinity, one that avoids tritheism on the one hand and Sabellianism (God is one person playing three parts in one story, like the late Peter Sellers) on the other, we are not likely to be accurate in our handling of texts that speak of God's plan of salvation, the team job in which Father, Son, and Holy Spirit work together to bring sinners to glory; nor are we likely to deal accurately with texts on the transactional reality of the atonement, the Son offering himself to the Father through the Spirit to bear the penalty due to us for our sins.

Or if we lack a biblical understanding of God's upholding of us as free and responsible decision-makers while overruling all our thoughts and actions according to his own will as to what shall be, we are not likely to deal accurately with texts about our life in Christ, where self-reliant activism is ruled out and God-dependent activity is to be the pattern, where the faith we exercise is the gift of God, where the indwelling Spirit energizes moral effort, and where we live and obey in awe and reverence, knowing that it is God who works in us to make us will and act as he wants us to do.

These are sample spheres of reality in which we need the help of theology to achieve exposition that is accurate and precise.

In the third place, only theology as described will secure *adequacy of application* when we preach. Theology offers a ready-made grid for making applications, and this is help that we need, for the theory of application is not on the whole well understood. The rhetoric, style and technique of application will of course vary from preacher to preacher, but the activity of application as such has an unvarying logic, which we can state thus: if this principle is truth from God, what difference should it make to our thinking, our resolves, our emotional attitudes, our motivation, and our view of our own spiritual state at this moment? More fully: if this principle is truth that God teaches and guarantees, then the following questions arise:

1. What particular judgments, and ways of thinking, does it require of us, and what habits of mind and particular opinions does it forbid us to entertain, and charge us to change if they are part of our life at present? (This is application to the mind.)

2. What particular actions, and what types of virtuous behaviour, does it require of us, and what vicious acts and habits does it forbid, and tell us to renounce herewith? (This is application to the will.)

3. What does it teach us to love, desire, hope for, insist on, and rejoice in, and what does it direct us to hate, abhor, fear, shrink from, and be sad at? (This is application to those emotionally freighted dispositional attitudes that the Puritans called 'affections'.)[13]

4. What encouragements are there here to embrace righteousness, or a particular aspect of righteousness, and persevere in it, and what discouragements are there here to dissuade us from lapsing into sinful habits and actions? (This is application at the level of motivation.)

5. How do we measure up to the requirements of this truth at this moment? And what are we going to do about our present shortcomings here, as self-scrutiny reveals them? And what conformity to the truth's requirements do we find in ourselves, for which we ought to thank God? And how do we propose to maintain and increase that conformity? (This is application for self-knowledge and self-assessment, as a step towards salutary adjustments of our life.)[14]

Clearly, not all the possible applications of each truth to all the different sorts of people one thinks one is preaching to (formalists, seekers, the self-righteous, the self-despairing, young Christians, veteran Christians, struggling Christians, and so on) can be made in every sermon, or it would never end! But the Puritans, the all-time specialists in application, gave something like half their preaching time to this task, and when one is preparing an expository sermon that is a good rule of thumb.

Comparison with the Puritans, the pioneer evangelicals, and expositors like J. C. Ryle and Arthur Pink, will soon convince us that the applicatory aspect of pastoral preaching today is underdeveloped.

One reason for this is that in an age like ours, in which the Scriptures are not well known or well respected, we are preoccupied with communicating biblical content and vindicating its divine authority, so that searching applications get crowded out. But a deeper reason is that, lacking a full-scale biblical and theological understanding of the Christian life – a systematic spirituality, as we might call it – we simply do not see what applications need to be made. Yet application is crucially important, partly because without it the preached Word will not humble and change people, and partly because it is in the process of application, as the Word is brought home to search the heart, that the sense of its divine authority becomes strongest, and the habit of submitting to it is most thoroughly formed. So the Westminster Directory was right to declare that the preacher

> is not to rest in general doctrine . . . but to bring it home to special use, by application to his hearers: which albeit it prove a work of great difficulty to himself, requiring much prudence, zeal, and meditation, and to the natural and corrupt man will be very unpleasant; yet he is to endeavour to perform it in such a manner, that his auditors may feel the word of God to be quick and powerful, and a discerner of the thoughts and intents of the heart . . .[15]

And we who preach today will do well to follow the Puritan lead at this point.

Conclusion

The thrust of this essay can be summed up thus: theology helps the preacher as the coach helps the tennis player, grooming and extending his performance by introducing him to the range of strokes that can be made and drilling him in the art of making them correctly. As the coach is the embodiment of decades of experience in playing tennis, so theology is the embodiment of centuries of study, debate, and interpretative interaction as the church has sought to understand the Scriptures. One can play tennis after a fashion without ever having been coached, and one can preach from the Bible after a fashion without ever having encountered serious theology in a serious way. But, just as one is likely to play better with coaching, so one is likely to preach better – more perceptively, more searchingly, more fruitfully – when helped by theology; and so the preacher who is theologically competent will, other things being equal, be more use to the church. That, in a nutshell, is what I had to say.

Notes

1. 'The exegete who is doing his work properly is forever asking the question: But what is the point? What is the author driving at? That is, he is always raising the question of the author's intent. At the same time, it is to be hoped that he is also asking questions about the content, questions of lexicography, syntax, background, and so forth. And, also, he is wary of overexegeting, for example, finding something that would stagger the author were he informed someone had found it in his writing, or building a theology upon the use of prepositions, or discovering meaning in what was *not* said.' Gordon Fee, 'Hermeneutics and Common Sense', in Roger R. Nicole and J. Ramsey Michaels (eds.), *Inerrancy and Common Sense* (Grand Rapids: Baker, 1980, pp. 178f.).

2. For the quadrilateral analysis, *cf.* the discussion by Edward Farley, *Theologia: The Fragmentation and Unity of Theological Education* (Philadelphia: Fortress, 1983).

3. Most textbooks of systematic theology follow this seven-part order; see, for instance, Millard J. Erickson, *Christian Theology*, 3 vols. (Grand Rapids: Baker, 1983–85); Bruce Milne, *Know the Truth*, (Leicester: IVP, 1982); Thomas C. Oden, *Systematic Theology*, 3 vols. (San Francisco: Harper and Row, 1986–92); James Montgomery Boice, *Foundations of the Christian Faith* (Downers Grove, Il.: IVP, 1986).

4. I met it quoted without a reference in Paul King Jewett, *Emil Brunner's Concept of Revelation* (London: James Clarke, 1954).

5. Ian Breward (ed.), *William Perkins* (Appleford: Sutton Courteney Press, 1970), p. 177.

6. This is how Calvin explains the role of his *Institutes*, from the second edition onward: 'It has been my purpose . . . to . . . instruct candidates in sacred theology for the reading of the divine Word . . . For I believe I have so embraced the sum of religion in all its parts, and have arranged it in such an order, that if anyone rightly grasps it, it will not be difficult for him to determine what he ought especially to seek in Scripture, and to what end he ought to relate its contents.' *Institutes of the Christian Religion*, trans. Ford Lewis Battles (Philadelphia: Westminster, 1967), I.4.

7. Article 20 of the Church of England's Thirty-nine Articles.

8. By Oswald Chambers, I believe, though I cannot track down the reference.

9. 'The Directory for the Publick Worship of God', in *The Confession of Faith* (Edinburgh: Banner of Truth, 1985), p. 380.

10. In the 1570s the preaching meetings that Queen Elizabeth I told Archbishop Grindal to suppress were called prophesyings; and the first Reformational textbook on preaching in England was *The Arte of Prophecying*, by William Perkins (*The Workes of that Famous Minister of Christ in the Universitie of Cambridge, Mr. William Perkins*, 1617, II, pp. 646–673; brief extract in Ian Breward, ed., *William Perkins*, pp. 325–349).

11. Donald Macleod, 'Preaching and Systematic Theology', in Samuel T. Logan (ed.), *The Preacher and Preaching* (Phillipsburg, NJ: Presbyterian and Reformed, 1986), p. 250.

12. *Ibid.*

13. The Puritan concept is precisely stated by Jonathan Edwards: *'Affection* is a word that, in its ordinary signification, seems to be something more extensive than *passion*, being used for all vigorous lively actings of the will or inclination . . . As all the exercises of inclination and will are concerned either in approving and liking, or disapproving and rejecting; so the affections are of two sorts; they are those by which the soul is carried out to what is in view, cleaving *to* it, or *seeking* it; or those by which it is averse *from* it, and *opposes* it. Of the former sort are *love, desire, hope, joy, gratitude, complacence.* Of the latter kind are *hatred, fear, anger, grief,* and such like . . .

'And there are some affections wherein there is a *composition* of each of the aforementioned kinds of actings of the will; as in the affection of *pity*, there is something of the *former kind*, towards the person suffering, and something of the *latter*, towards what he suffers. And so in *zeal*, there is in it high *approbation* of some person or thing, together with vigorous *opposition* to what is conceived to be contrary to it.' *A Treatise concerning Religious Affections*, in vol I of *The Works of Jonathan Edwards*, ed. H. Hickman (Edinburgh: Banner of Truth, 1974), p. 237.

14. For more discussion of application, see J. I. Packer, 'Method: Speaking for God', in Richard Allen Bodey (ed.), *Inside the Sermon* (Grand Rapids: Baker, 1990), pp. 188–190.

15. *The Confession of Faith*, p. 380.

7

The preacher as pastor

The Shepherd's care

Edmund P. Clowney

Pastoral preaching may be defined narrowly to describe a variety of Christian preaching, to be contrasted with evangelistic preaching or kerygmatic proclamation. Describing the teaching offices in the church, the apostle Paul differentiates between evangelists and those who are pastors and teachers (Eph. 4:11). Even pastors and teachers, although closely linked, are apparently distinguishable. John Calvin, mindful of his own ministry, recognized the distinct calling of the teacher among those who are ministers of the Word.[1]

Pastoring and the preacher

In these days of medical specialization we are not surprised to find that spiritual specialization has grown as well. Large churches now have a staff of associate or assistant pastors serving with a senior pastor. Such pastors are given specific charges: the educational work of the church, its evangelistic programme, or its counselling ministry. Some job descriptions are even more specific, focused on particular groups as defined by age, ethnic background, vocation, or physical and financial needs.

In the half century and more since my own days as a theological student, both the growth of megachurches and the expansion of counselling seem to have changed the concept of pastoral care. My professor of practical theology, R. B. Kuiper, taught the cure of souls as the duty of every pastor, and advised us that the top limit for congregational size was 250 families or about 300 communicant members, since a pastor could not provide adequate pastoral care for a larger flock. Congregations that reach the limit should set about establishing daughter churches. Professor Kuiper also admired the pastoral care that Calvin developed in Geneva, and particularly the programme of annual visits by a minister and elder in the households of the church to enquire into their spiritual state. (We did not then examine the congregational structure in the city of Geneva, or the number of communicants worshipping at St Peter's in Calvin's day.)

One great change in the understanding of pastoral care has been a clearer recognition of the functioning of the whole body of Christ. Spiritual gifts are not the sole possession of the clergy, nor can any minister alone provide the whole spiritual care of even the smallest of flocks. The whole body 'grows and builds itself up in love, as each part does its work' (Eph. 4:16). Increasingly, ministers of the Word have come to think of themselves as coaches, training the members to carry on the work of ministry.

Understanding the spiritual contribution of every church member to the life of the body has brought renewal to many churches, large and small. Yet we must also remember how Paul begins the passage in which he speaks of the functioning of each member of the body. To each one of us grace has been given as Christ apportioned it (Eph. 4:7). But when the apostle describes the gifts that the ascended Christ has given, he does not speak of gifts in the abstract, but of apostles, prophets, evangelists, pastors and teachers. Those who minister the Word of God labour for the perfecting of the saints; Paul poured himself out to present the church as a pure virgin to Christ (2 Cor. 11:2), and every Christian perfect in Christ (Col. 1:28f.). Much as we rejoice in the counselling that Christians receive in small group fellowships and through Christian counsellors, we have good reason to hope that pastors will not delegate to others their pastoring function, or suppose that their ministry of the Word can be limited to textual exposition. If the pastor is to coach others, he cannot call plays from the sidelines. He must be a playing coach, instructing by example as well as by word. Indeed, if team images from sports are to be used, the pastor is not so much a coach as a key player: the quarterback in American football, or the basketball centre. It is possible to speak of pastoral preaching as one aspect of the ministry of the Word, but it is not possible to think of a ministry of the Word that is not fundamentally pastoral. The Word that drives us to the pulpit drives us to face the needs of the people of God gathered before us.

The art of pastoral preaching

Yet to say that pastoral concern is necessary for preaching may be too mild an acknowledgment by far. Is not pastoral concern the *whole* purpose of preaching? Jay Adams, who has yet to bury a truth under a bushel of qualifications, does not hesitate to affirm that purpose.[2] He deplores the approach, drawn from late medieval scholasticism, that would find the theme of a text, expound the theme under two or three divisions, then raise the question of the application or 'uses' of what has been explained. Adams argues that the whole approach is wrong. Preachers are not lecturers rising to discuss the teaching of a passage in the third person. They are addressing people, communicating with them for a purpose. Their task is to find the purpose for which the scriptural passage was written, and shape the whole message to accomplish that same purpose in the lives of the hearers of the sermon.

Dr Adams is quite right about the background of homiletical theory in medieval scholasticism. Thomas Marie Charland OP, in *Artes Praedicandi*,[3] has described the preaching manuals of the thirteenth and fourteenth centuries, and the development of the art of preaching that they trace.[4] They were designed to guide the preaching in Latin that was done in the universities; indeed the spread of the manuals corresponded with the development of the universities.[5] Popular preaching, such as might be done on feast days, was not to be held to such exacting standards. The figure of a tree and its branches was a favourite image for medieval homiletics. The text is at the root of the sermon, the theme is its trunk, and divides into branches; these subdivide into further branches as the sermon develops. At the last come the flowers and fruits borne by the twigs of subdivisions. Here the practical 'fruit' of the sermon appears. The difficulty is that sermonic trees may well incur the judgment the Saviour pronounced on the barren fig tree; they may be full of branches and leaves, but lack fruit. Medieval university preaching was labour-intensive: the development of the divisions required meticulous attention, confirming authorities had to be discovered for each step (from the Fathers, or from other scriptures); the interrelation of subdivisions had to be designed, and the headings put into rhyme to be fixed in memory. Little time or attention would remain for the final trimming of the tree with fruit.

The *Artes* manuals contain some revealing asides. At one point

Thomas Waleys of Oxford observes that while it is rhetorically essential to keep to the main theme of the sermon, a digression would be justified for the sake of edifying the hearers: 'The exigencies of human rhetoric must yield to the good of souls, the goal of preaching.'[6] If, in the course of preaching, a thought came to him that might stir the devotion of the hearers, it would be wrong to suppress it for the sake of rhetorical consistency. That would verge on profanation, for it would be to sacrifice the honour of God and the benefit of one's neighbour to a rhetorical curiosity. 'The supreme art of the preacher consists in edifying the people and provoking them to good works.'[7]

In the discussion of principles for forming divisions of the theme, the manuals pointed out that the divisions may derive from the words of the text itself, or from some outside consideration. Divisions from outside are easier for common people to grasp, it is said, while preachers to university audiences could expect their learned hearers to appreciate the neater precision of using only the words of the text. For example, a sermon on the text 'The LORD is my light and my salvation' (Ps. 27:1) could be organized by using this consideration from outside the text: sin has inflicted a double evil: ignorance has darkened our *knowing*, and infirmity has crippled our *acting*. The sermon could then show that as Light, God removes our ignorance; and, as Salvation, he delivers us from our weakness.

The Reformation made preaching popular, and was swept forward by preaching. Crowds gathered to hear Luther; the Great Church of Zurich was packed with listeners attending to the biblical preaching of Zwingli. Philip Melanchthon revised his text on classical rhetoric for training preachers;[8] unfortunately it was this book that went through many editions rather than another text on preaching that he wrote a few years later.[9] In the later work he departed from classical models to define preaching in more biblical categories: for instruction; for inciting to faith; and for exhortation in morality. Here the purposes of preaching were made definitive of sermon styles.

The father of Reformed homiletics was Andreas Gerhard (1511–1564), called Hyperius from his birthplace in Ypres in Flanders. Hyperius traced the relationships and differences between classical rhetoric and preaching. Augustine had shown that the preacher must face many of the same problems as the orator: he must research his material, organize it, give it spoken form, and present it in delivery. Styles of preaching will at times, therefore, resemble other styles of public discourse. The threefold aim of the orator is not entirely out of place for the preacher: to instruct, to delight, and to influence (*docere, delectare, flectere*). But Hyperius traced the distinctiveness of preaching to its content and form, and sought his modes in Scripture. He found them in 2 Timothy 3:16 and Romans 15:4. Preaching uses Scripture for the purposes for which it is given: for teaching, reproof, instruction, correction and comfort. Preaching brings us the understanding found in Scripture, its direction for our practice, and its encouragement for our hearts.

In spite of so firm a grounding in the pastoral form of preaching, the pulpits of Reformed churches still stood in the shadows of scholastic precedents. Much later, Abraham Kuyper had to warn that the application of Scripture is not like a little skiff towed behind a great ship (or we might say, a Volkswagen Beetle behind a container lorry!). At the worst, application is made not only an arbitrary addition to a biblical lecture, but a standard one at that. The evangelical organist slips forward to play the closing hymn when she hears the pastor slide into those familiar final formulas pleading for faith and consecration.

Changes great and small can help to recover the pastoral dimension of preaching, and with it preaching itself as a ministry of the Word of God. Structuring a sermon with its purpose in view is as biblical as it is sound communication. Adams does well to remind preachers, too, not to be afraid to address a congregation in the second person (although not to the exclusion of the first person plural, as the epistles of Paul instruct us). Yet the greatest change needed is also the deepest: the prayerful renewal of the preacher's concern for those committed to his care.

The fire of pastoral preaching

Here we feel the reproof of the apostle Paul. We know that his calling was not to build where others had laboured, but to lay the foundations of Christian faith among the Gentiles, proclaiming Jesus Christ where his name had not been known (Rom. 15:20). Paul was a missionary, an apostolic evangelist, pointed always toward the horizons of his vast area of ministry. Further, the apostle was looking for the return of his Lord in the glory of his kingdom. He assured his converts that when they saw the Lord they would bear his likeness (1 Cor. 15:49). Pressing toward the end of the age and the limits of the empire, Paul might be expected to show little concern for the nurture of his converts. He had won them to the Lord; he had committed them to the Lord; could he not await the day when they would be made like the Lord? Let others build where he had laid the foundation, and let them be sure to labour in gold, silver, and precious stones. He was the master builder; let them finish the job.

Yet that would be to misunderstand the apostle completely. The letters by which we know him are fiercely eloquent with Paul's desire to provide everything needful for the nurture of the churches. Resolved to confirm his converts, he followed the road back into the very places that he had barely escaped with his life. Stoned at Lystra, and restored by Christ's power, he got to his feet and walked back into the city, before going on to Derbe. Not satisfied with that, he returned again to Lystra and the other centres of persecution, 'strengthening the disciples and encouraging them to remain true to the faith. "We must go through many hardships to enter the kingdom of God"' (Acts 14:22).

Paul writes the manifesto that drove him to ceaseless travel and labour, shipwrecks, beatings and imprisonment:

> We proclaim him, admonishing and teaching everyone with all wisdom, so that we may present everyone perfect in Christ. To this end I labour, struggling with all his energy, which so powerfully works in me. (Col. 1:28–29)

That apostolic concern is the fire of pastoral preaching. Apart from that burning zeal and the prayer and dedication that it produces, the pastoral office cannot be fulfilled. It may seem curious that the apostle who so fully trusted in the Lord's grace should labour so desperately for the perfecting of the saints. But it was the love of Christ that constrained him to serve as a faithful shepherd of Christ's flock. Preachers who cultivate a professional stance to the pastorate as a career will never understand the meaning of the words, 'Zeal for your house will consume me' (Jn. 2:17).

When Jesus restored the apostle Peter to his pastoral duties after the resurrection, he examined him three times on one point: 'Do you love me?' Peter's pride had been shorn away by his denials; no longer would he pretend to be the one disciple who would always remain true. Indeed, at the last, Peter affirmed his love, not because *he* knew it, but because the Lord knew it. The Lord's heart-searching revealed Peter's love to prepare for the renewal of Peter's pastoral charge. Jesus called him to feed and tend his sheep and to care for the lambs of the flock. For Peter as for Paul, it is love for Christ that must qualify the pastor. This is true, not only because only love for Christ will prove sufficient motivation for bearing the burdens of pastoral care, but also because pastoral ministry is itself a ministry of the love of Christ.

In this lies the key to pastoral counselling and to pastoral preaching. A recent book on pastoral preaching indirectly shows the need for an approach centred on Jesus Christ. J. Randall Nichols is a practising psychotherapist, a preacher and a teacher of preaching. His book *The Restoring Word: Preaching as Pastoral Communication*[10] seeks to mark the road in a field that he believes needs fresh analysis. Since he brings together both long clinical and preaching experience, his qualifications commend him. His own desire for openness and honesty makes him an engaging writer. Yet his analysis all hangs on the modern assumption that religious language, 'God-talk', is *interpretative* rather than *descriptive*.[11] It does not speak of objective realities, but projects concepts with meaning for life. There are no 'acts of God' to be objectively described, nor are there 'words of God' to be proclaimed. There is only a sense of meaningfulness in the impact of the ineffable mysteriousness of our experience, which we see as the inbreaking of the transcendent. In short, although Nichols speaks of proclamation and teaching as forms of preaching, he has reduced preaching to *therapeia*. The preacher must learn the stance of 'interpretative acceptance' that accords with the meaning of religious language, and not destroy it by sprinkling in 'oughts' and 'shoulds' that destroy the permissive relationship in which learning and growth are possible.[12]

He says that the pulpit, like the therapist's office, is a kind of sanctuary, a refuge from the pressures and responsibilities of daily life, where it is possible to step outside of the daily demands and reflect on them; where it will be recognized that emotions have no moral quality, and we will not be blamed for our feelings, but have the freedom to express them.

From his perspective, fundamentalist Christianity does all the wrong things, loading guilt-trips on people, denouncing them for what they can't help, and offering threats in the place of acceptance.

Therapeutic pastors, however, are not evangelists pointing out the way to life; they are rather 'trail-guides' who may have some experience to share from having been down the road before, and may offer advice on how to read the map. Other roles that Nichols proposes are fallen heroes, fellow strap-hanging commuters, even hostages 'whose message is basically "I can't get out of this mess, but maybe you can."'[13] To identify the conflict, even while losing the struggle, is 'a self-enacting strength with value of its own.'

No doubt there is some appeal in this Charlie Brown role for the pastor, certainly when contrasted with the pose of a self-righteous and hypocritical Elmer Gantry, but it is a web of despair stretched across the dark void where the gospel has been removed. What is missing from the picture, or rather, *who* is missing from the picture in this sad therapy, is the living Saviour, Jesus Christ, the great Shepherd of the sheep.

Pastoral preaching is indeed therapeutic, but its power does not come from the preacher, or from his experiences down the road. The healing comes from Jesus, and from the objective reality of who he is, and what he has done, and continues to do for our salvation. The gospel is good news: the news that the living God has become incarnate, and that his salvation is as real as his cross and the rock tomb that stood empty on Easter morning. The gospel message is not that 'God so loved the world that he inspired a certain Jew to teach that there was a good deal to be said for loving one another.'[14] The gospel does include an imperative, the imperative to believe in the Son of God, but the imperative is grounded in the indicative: that he died for our sins and rose for our salvation so that we might look to him and live. Precisely the preaching that the modern mind rejects as mythical is the preaching that is the power of God to salvation.

The Pastor whom we preach

To deal with men and women pastorally, we must bring them to the Pastor. 'The LORD is my Shepherd, I shall not want.' In our lostness we have wandered far from the Lord, but Jesus came to seek and to save that which was lost. He comes to us, as he came to the house of Zaccheus, bringing salvation with him, for it is his presence that we had lost. We were like sheep going astray (Is. 53:6), 'but now you have returned to the Shepherd and Overseer of your souls' (1 Pet. 2:25). Jesus who has brought us back to his fold provides for our needs. He leads us into green pastures and provides for us the very bread of heaven. The nourishment that Christ provides is sacramentally given in the communion feast, but always with his Word. That which Christ gives is himself. The metaphor of food describes the personal fellowship that is established by his Spirit in our hearts. It is this interpersonal experience that is advanced through the describing of Christ and his benefits so that believers may lay hold on him by faith.

The Shepherd who provides spiritual nourishment also gives refreshment and rest, for he leads us by still waters and restores our souls. The insight is valid that restorative healing requires sanctuary, a drawing apart from the storms of life, its fears and threats, to a place of acceptance and peace. No privileged client relationship, however, can match the acceptance of Jesus Christ. His enemies accused him of being a friend of tax-collectors and sinners. He was not ashamed of harlots and drew his disciples from among such people. Yet he did not condone sin; he forgave it. He could do so, for he came for that purpose: not to bring the judgment but to bear it; not to thrust with the spear of divine vindication, but to receive the spear-thrust in his side. Only so might sinners be made children of God.

The Bible describes the atonement in the language of love. Christ, who loved his own that were in the world, loved them to the end (Jn. 13:1). When there was no time or space or spreading billions of galaxies, in what we must think of as the time before time, there was love, for God the Son was in the embrace of God the Father (Jn. 1:18). But John 3:16 does not say that the Father so loved the Son that he gave him the world (see Jn. 3:35). It says that God so loved the world that he gave his only begotten Son. The point is not how big the world is, as though God could not bear to be without it; the point is how bad the world is, how deserving of God's judgment in its rebellion and sin. When Paul describes that love of God for his enemies, he says that this is the love that is poured out in our hearts by the Holy Spirit who is given to us (Rom. 5:5). The healing power of that love is what mends broken hearts and gives power to the faint. What access do sinners have to such abundance of healing grace? The answer, of course, is again to be found in Jesus Christ alone.

The Shepherd who provides nourishment and refreshment also leads his flock. 'He tends his flock like a shepherd: he gathers the lambs in his arms and carries them close to his heart; he gently leads those that have young' (Is. 40:11). The Lord who led Israel through the desert again leads his people through times of testing. He leads them by the way that he has gone, for the sheep follow the Shepherd, walking in his steps (1 Pet. 2:21). They follow him, for they know his voice. The metaphor again points us to the instruction of Scripture and the preaching of the Word of Christ, for so are Christians taught in the wisdom of the Spirit as they follow Christ. They learn that we do not live by bread alone in our journey, but by every word that proceeds from the Lord (Dt. 8:3): the word of his commandment of love (Dt. 6:4–5), but also the word of his direction (Dt. 8:2) in the life curriculum by which he leads us to the final rest.

Along the way that the Shepherd leads, his rod and staff provide protection. He has vanquished the principalities and powers that would delude and oppress us. We need fear no evil, for he is with us. In the deadly darkness, when only he can be with us, he will not forsake us. His goodness and mercy not only follow us; they pursue us, for they are the evidence of his own presence, who is the Good Shepherd, who gave his life for the sheep.

> For I am convinced that neither death nor life, neither angels nor demons, neither the present nor the future, nor any powers, neither height nor depth, nor anything else in all creation, will be able to separate us from the love of God that is in Christ Jesus our Lord (Rom. 8:38f.).

What gospel preacher does not know these things? Indeed, what Christian has not sought and shared the comfort of knowing that 'the LORD is my Shepherd'? Yet no conviction is more crucial for effective pastoral preaching. Let the preacher recover the simple recognition that he introduces another; that he is the friend of the bridegroom, that Christ must increase and he decrease. The Lord does equip you with many gifts and graces for your calling; it is of his Spirit that you have genuine love for your people, that you can compassionately bear with the foolish and the stubborn, and yearn to recover the wayward. But the hope of all pastoral care rests with the Shepherd himself. Your compassion cannot draw them, nor can your hand guide them or your rod and staff correct them. The work of pastoral preaching is to present Jesus Christ from all the Scriptures, in all the glory of his person and work.

Does this mean that pastoral preaching can be reduced to the simplest outlines of the gospel, so that little instruction is needed except the basic message of the cross? Or, to put the matter even more baldly, does the shepherding of Christ himself mean that our proclamation may be made in a 'take it or leave it' fashion, since the work of shepherding must ultimately be his? The apostle Paul's reaction again shows us how far this is from the truth. Hear him as he pleads with the Galatians not to forsake the gospel they heard: 'My dear children, for whom I am again in the pains of childbirth until Christ is formed in you, how I wish I could be with you now and change my tone, because I am perplexed about you!' (Gal. 4:19).

The power of Christ-directed preaching

Actually, the basic understanding of pastoral preaching, that Christ is the Pastor, also directs the under-shepherd in caring for his flock. Apart from that conviction, every pastor must cry, 'Who is equal to such a task?' (2 Cor. 2:16). To be an aroma of life to some, but the very odour of death to others – who can be adequate for such a ministry? Our own sufficiency must be found in him who is the Shepherd, calling his own sheep by name. The key to pastoral ministry must be that 'we do not preach ourselves, but Jesus Christ as Lord, and ourselves as your servants for Jesus' sake' (2 Cor. 4:5). The faithful under-shepherd does identify with the Lord he serves. He feels the burden of speaking with the tenderness that will understand, but with the firmness that will correct and restore. Yet the concern of the pastor is transformed by the fact that it is concern for the relation of the congregation to Christ, not to himself. Let that be forgotten, and pastoral concern immediately changes to a form of manipulation, of empire-building, of self-gratification.

The growth in holiness for which pastoral preaching labours is growth in likeness to Christ, who is the fulfilment of the law to believers. The law of God marks out what is pleasing to God; it defines the way of life in which the believer walks. Jesus did not discard that law; he taught the depth of it in an obedience that proceeds from the heart. He showed how it all hangs on the great commandment to love God with all one's heart, soul, strength and mind, and on the other commandment that is like it and flows from it: to love one's neighbour as one's self. Jesus kept the law for us, and in his keeping of it, he showed us the depth of the meaning of love that we could not imagine: love that does not ask, 'Who is my neighbour? How many people must I love?' Rather, the love of Christ given to us asks, 'To whom may I be a neighbour? To whom may I show what has been shown to me, the love of compassion, God's love in Jesus Christ?'

This is the Christian ethic that transforms marriages, reconciles parents and children, heals bitter hatred: it is love for our enemies, like God's love for us, once his enemies. Nothing could be more evident than that we ourselves cannot demand the very love that cannot be demanded – the freely given love of grace. Only through the knowledge of Jesus Christ, revealed through the work of his Spirit, can one desire to be like him, to love because he first loved us. To hold up that standard of holy love, the love that fulfills the law, is to hold up Jesus Christ. Pastoral preaching examines all the riches of the biblical revelation of Christ; it traces the history of God's redemptive grace in the Old Testament to show how God's Word and God's work reveal grace for grace (Jn. 1:16f., AV): the grace by which God proclaimed to Moses his Name as the 'compassionate and gracious God' (Ex. 34:6), and the grace that appeared when the Word became flesh and tabernacled among us – the true Tabernacle – and we saw his glory, full of grace and truth (Jn. 1:14). The wisdom literature of the Old Testament points us to the resolution of the problems of wisdom in the call of him who is wisdom incarnate: 'Take my yoke upon you and learn from me' (Mt. 11:29). He who is the Son alone knows the Father, and can reveal him, just as only the Father knows him, and can reveal him. The prophets foretold his coming, his glory, and his saving work; the Psalms anticipate the One who is David's greater Son, the singing Saviour. Every aspect of the revelation of Christ in the Bible is rich in strengthening faith, in lifting our eyes to see Jesus, the Shepherd, who restores our souls. All preaching will be pastoral if it centres as it must on Jesus Christ.

Notes

1. John Calvin, *Sermons on Ephesians* (London: Banner of Truth, 1973), p. 365.

2. Jay E. Adams, *Preaching With Purpose: The Urgent Task of Homiletics* (Grand Rapids: Zondervan, 1982).

3. *Artes Praedicandi: contribution à l'histoire de la rhétorique au moyen age* (Ottawa: Institut d'Études Médiévales, 1936).

4. Especially those of Thomas Waleys and of Robert de Basevorn, who compares the methods of Oxford with those of Paris.

5. *Artes Praedicandi*, p. 110.

6. *Ibid.*, p. 136.

7. *Ibid.*, p. 136.

8. *Elements Rhetorices*, 1531.

9. *Dissertatio de officio concionatoris*, 1537.

10. San Francisco: Harper and Row, 1987.

11. *The Restoring Word*, pp. 50f. Nichols does say 'more' interpretative than descriptive, but his elaboration of the point makes it evident that religious language functions interpretatively: to assign meaning to our experience.

12. *Ibid.*, p. 25.

13. *Ibid.*, p. 120.

14. As F. D. Coggan summarized the older liberalism in *The Ministry of the Word: The New Testament Concept of Preaching, and its Relevance for To-day* (London: Canterbury Press, 1945), p. 77.

III

8

Preaching that grows the church

Frank J. Retief

There is a real difference between drawing a crowd and building a church.

A crowd may be drawn by oratory and entranced by verbal fireworks. Some persons are naturally gifted speakers with an instinctive ability to hold audiences spellbound. Among them are to be found some preachers.[1] Yet when the content of their sermons is analysed it becomes clear that they are orators rather than preachers of 'the whole will of God' (Acts 20:27).

Nor is there any expected connection between moral character and oratorical ability. The brilliant orator, David Lloyd-George, who served as Prime Minister of Great Britain from 1916 to 1922, was a notorious philanderer.

What makes preaching different from oratory and acting is that it is required to be rooted in a life of personal godliness (see 1 Tim. 4:12–13). It is not aimed at growing a church by the tricks of rhetoric, but directed to pointing people to Christ the only Saviour of sinners. It is not the putting on of an act, but the proclaiming of the good news of forgiveness of sins through the crucified and risen Christ.

What then are the important elements in preaching that builds a church? How are preachers of the gospel to minister so that God is honoured, Christ is truly presented as the Saviour of sinners and souls are edified? I venture here to set out certain principles, recognizing that no-one can hope adequately to put down on paper the do's and don'ts of public Christian ministry. We are all so different in gifts and temperaments. God in his glorious sovereignty often confounds us all by using the most unexpected instruments to do his work. Those who do all the right things often see little blessing, while others who seem to have little to commend them sometimes see God at work. Nevertheless, I suggest that there are certain important factors to bear in mind for a ministry that builds the church.

The preacher before God

Preaching at an ordination service in 1841, the celebrated Robert Murray M'Cheyne chose as his text 2 Timothy 4:1–2. He made the point that the preacher stands before God as a minister of the gospel. This is true in two ways. First, the minister remembers that he is a sinner saved by grace and thus is an example to his hearers of the very salvation he is proclaiming. Secondly, he stands before God as a servant and is conscious of the eye of his divine Master upon him.[2]

M'Cheyne emphasized that preachers should *feel* the presence of the Saviour.[3] This so often seemed to be the experience of the great preachers of old. Read through the biographies of Whitefield or Wesley and see how often they felt 'strengthened' or 'enlarged' while preaching. This element of divine help, the sense of God's presence, needs to be given to us again. And we need to pray for such help, believing that we shall receive it.

But surely, if this is to be our experience, there must be an integrity in our daily walk with God. In his most helpful booklet *What's Wrong with Preaching Today?* Al Martin comments:

> The principle is this: that unless we would degrade preaching to a mere elocutionary art, we must never forget that the soil out of which powerful preaching grows is the preacher's own life. This is what makes the art of preaching different from all other arts of communication. A well-known actress may be famous for her 'moral' escapades. She may live like a common harlot. Yet she can enter the theatre at eight o'clock on a Wednesday night and play the role of Joan of Arc in such a way as to move the entire audience to tears. The way

126

in which she lives may have no direct relationship with the exercising of her professional art.[4]

Preaching is different from every other performance. True preaching issues out of a heart aflame with love for God and utterly convinced of the truthfulness of the gospel. But preaching is not a mere physical act, or the exercise of certain skills. It is true that the pulpit can become a stage where the preacher puts on a performance. But if preaching is to be true preaching, it must be rooted in the integrity of the spiritual life of the preacher.

Our personal relationship with God must be kept unclouded for the pulpit. How can we preach if our wives or children are silently crying 'Hypocrite!' while they listen to us? We must maintain a witness in our own homes before we presume to 'manage' the house of God (1 Tim. 3:5).

There must be a 'blamelessness' before there can be an effective ministry (1 Tim. 3:2; Tit. 1:6). The man must be prepared before God before the message comes with power from his lips. The very least we can expect from our preachers is a personal experience of saving grace, a clear conviction that the Christian gospel is authoritative and that Christ is unique, and a personal walk with God that enables the Holy Spirit to use the preacher as an instrument of blessing.

To quote M'Cheyne:

> To stand at his feet; in his family; in his pavilion; oh, believers, it is then we get above the billows! The applause of men, the rage and contempt of men, then pass by us like the idle wind which we regard not. Thus is a minister like a rock in the ocean; the mountain billows dash upon its brow, and yet it stands unshaken.[5]

A sense of eternity

Every time the Word of God is preached, the preacher and his audience meet in the presence of God: he to preach and to be accountable to God for what he says, and they to hear and to be accountable for how they hear. M'Cheyne reminds us of another day when the minister will meet his flock again – before the throne of the Lord Jesus on the day of judgment.[6] Of all the solemn occasions of meeting on this earth, none can be compared to the solemnity of that day when we preachers give an account with either joy over those who receive the gospel or grief over those who neglected it.

If only we could recapture the sense that we are working toward another world and that the consequences of our preaching are eternal!

How it would affect our preparation, praying, frame of mind and actual delivery. If we could see eternity with the eye of faith, surely our passion and zeal would be stirred up. How careful we would be that all we say about the gospel is true, and how jealous we would be for the uniqueness of our message!

There is a great deal to do in the normal course of pastoral work. We must visit the people and discern where their hearts are. We must deal with their problems, doubts, queries and struggles. We must visit the sick, help to relieve the poor, clothe the naked. All these are needed, but the great work to which we are called is to preach the Word. Woe betide us if we allow this great task to become secondary! And it will, if we lose sight of the fact that we work before the one who is the judge of the living and the dead.

We must keep before us the great picture of a countless multitude whose robes have been washed in the blood of the Lamb (Rev. 7:14). They have all come out of the great tribulation. In other words, they have come out of the world of sin and rebellion against God, where they encountered opposition, suffering and persecution. The realm of light and glory is our final destination. We must work and preach with that in mind. The awful consequences of rejecting Christ must ever be uppermost in our preaching and teaching so that a sense of urgency is maintained in our delivery.

One night Bramwell Booth, son of the famous founder of the Salvation Army, found the old general pacing up and down his room with a wet towel around his head to alleviate a headache. 'Ought you not to be asleep?' Bramwell asked.

'No, I am thinking,' said William Booth, shaking his head. Then, placing his hands on his son's shoulders, he said, 'Bramwell, I am thinking about the people's sins. What will they do with their sins?'[7]

That kind of ache, burden, and awareness of eternal consequences must be sensed in our preaching. This is not something that can be obtained at a college. It must be planted in our hearts with the divine call to preach. In fact, I wonder if people who do not have the 'ache of eternity' are really called to preach the gospel or to build a church.

In his heart-warming book *Christian Leaders of the 18th Century*, Bishop J. C. Ryle writes about Daniel Rowland, the famous Welsh preacher. He quotes a description of his preaching as given by an eyewitness, a fellow preacher, Christmas Evans.

> There was such a vehement invisible flame in his ministry, as effectually drove away the careless, worldly, dead spirit; and people so awakened drew nigh as it were to the bright cloud – to Christ, to Moses, and Elias – eternity and its amazing realities rushing into their minds.[8]

Biblical preaching

It should be a given that the Bible is our textbook. Indeed, it *is* a given in many churches today. Sadly, it is not so in all churches. What have we possibly got to offer as preachers of God's Word if God's Word is not what we preach? We do not have a right to obtain our material from the world of psychology, politics, literature, science or anywhere else. To be sure, we may plunder all those areas (and more) to illustrate and reinforce the truth of the Bible, but they may not replace the Bible as our source of authority. It is true that the God of the Bible is the God of all creation, and thus there is a sense in which we can trace his presence in all the world around us. It is also true that biblical preaching may have an impact in all these fields, but that is by way of application, not as the main theme of our message.

The main theme of the Bible is the gospel. Both Old and New Testaments are about God's redeeming acts. All the Bible points to God's final act of redemption in Christ. Therefore the Bible is all about Christ. The Old Testament builds up to the cross. The gospel centres on Christ, his character, deeds, words, death, resurrection, and ascension to the Father's right hand. In Acts, the epistles and Revelation the meaning of his life, death and resurrection is fleshed out. This must be our message.

Speaking about Daniel Rowland, J. C. Ryle comments:

> The blood, the sacrifice, the righteousness, the kindness, the patience, the saving grace, the example, the greatness of the Lord Jesus are subjects which appear to run through every sermon, and to crop up at every turn. It seems as if the preacher could never say enough about his Master and was never weary of commending him to his hearers . . . Here I suspect was precisely the great secret of Rowland's power. A ministry full of the Lord Jesus is exactly the sort of ministry that I should expect God to bless. Christ-honouring sermons are just the sermons that the Holy Spirit seals with success.[9]

When it comes to biblical preaching, however, we must be careful to make it *expository* biblical preaching. Evangelical preaching often falls into two camps. The one can be labelled as *exhortatory*. The preacher gathers up great biblical themes or principles and exhorts his hearers by applying the themes to them. There is nothing wrong with this kind of preaching. Many of the men God used in past times of revival were untrained laymen who could do little else but exhort. Often evangelistic preaching takes this form because the audiences are transitory or have no biblical foundation to build upon. This kind of preaching is often the primary way of breaking into a new situation. In addition, the use of television lends itself to this style of preaching. In South Africa the national television service opens and closes with a three-minute devotional service. What can one say in three minutes? A brief word of exhortation is all that can be offered.

Having said that, I must go on to say that in my opinion exhortatory preaching will never build a church. In order to build a congregation and to see it grow, much more content is needed. Biblical illiteracy will never be expelled by a constant diet of exhortations. There must be exposition. By this I mean the regular, thoughtful, systematic and simple explaining of a Bible book or passage. We have no right to make the Bible say what *we* want it to say or what we may deem necessary for our audience at any given time. The Bible must be allowed to speak for itself. That is the way to spiritual growth. The call back to expository teaching issued by the Proclamation Trust is exactly what is needed in our biblically ignorant age. Who will teach the masses the Bible if we preachers do not? And how can they ever learn if all they are given are large doses of general principles? They need to know what the distinctive message of each of the biblical books is all about! There may be numerous ways of doing this, of course. Apart from Sunday preaching, all sorts of study groups can be devised to meet the needs of any church. But it must be done. Charles Haddon Spurgeon put it like this:

> If people are to be saved by a discourse, it must contain at least some measure of knowledge. There must be light as well as fire. Some preachers are all light and no fire, and others are all fire and no light; what we want is both fire and light. I do not judge those brethren who are all fire and fury; but I wish they had a little more knowledge of what they talk about, and I think it would be well if they did not begin quite so soon to preach what they hardly understand themselves. It is a fine thing to stand up in the street, and cry 'Believe! Believe! Believe! Believe! Believe!' Yes, my dear soul, but what have we to believe? What is all this noise about? . . .
>
> The sermons that are most likely to convert people seem to me to be those that are full of truth: truth about the fall, truth about the law, truth about human nature, and its alienation from God, truth about Jesus Christ, truth about the Holy Spirit, truth about the Everlasting Father, truth about the new birth, truth about obedience to God, and how we learn it, and all such great verities. Tell your hearers something, dear brethren, whenever you preach, tell them something, tell them something![10]

Applicatory preaching

It seems to me that if our preaching is to build the church of God, the people listening to us need to have a sense that the Bible passage we are expounding has something to say to them, today. Some preachers are diffident about being too applicatory in their preaching. I have heard it said that members of the congregation are quite able to work out the application for themselves and that it is an insult to assume otherwise. Other preachers feel that great offence may be caused if lessons are applied too directly. Still others feel that all we need to do is proclaim the meaning of the text and the Holy Spirit will apply the meaning to the individual. While there are no doubt elements of truth in all these reactions I nevertheless believe they are largely mistaken. We must obviously avoid being offensive and crude in our applications. It is true too that, like others, I have sometimes cringed as I heard preachers applying their message in a judgmental and condemning manner. But the mistakes or blunders of others must not deter us from seeking out and confronting the consciences of our hearers.

To get an idea of how to confront people's consciences, one can hardly do better than read the life of William Booth. I do not suggest that the methods and approaches which the Salvation Army used 120 years ago are sufficient for today; nevertheless, there was in those days a boldness and an instinct for evangelism that gave those evangelists a resourcefulness in communication and a quick wit that enabled them to hold their own among the rough crowds that gathered round them. In his excellent biography of Booth, *The General Next to God*, Richard Collier illustrates the need to be plain in our preaching and application.

> More dramatic still was the reaction of a guilty citizen at Birmingham's Town Hall. With mounting intensity Booth was portraying the dilemma of a seducer on Judgement Day: 'Here she comes – the woman he seduced! Her golden hair is falling over her shoulders – she is screaming, "That is the man! That is the man!"' Suddenly to the horror of all, a voice from the gallery cried in torment, 'My God – he means me!' Then, with an appalling crash, he leaped clean over the balcony to the floor of the hall, stumbling miraculously unhurt up the aisle to collapse at the Penitent-form.[11]

Although many of us may not be comfortable with such rough and ready tactics, nevertheless I venture to suggest that the true preacher will find ways of making his message applicable. There must be an element in our preaching that carries the voice of Nathan and says, 'You are the man.' Sooner or later our hearers must say to themselves,

'He means *me*.' If not, what on earth are we accomplishing?

I realize that different audiences and situations call for different approaches. While we may be placed in different ministerial situations, if we are preachers at all, we must be governed by the eternal consequences of what we are doing. Surely our gospel instincts will find a way of connecting what we are saying with the consciences of our hearers. The people must be woken up. We must seek in our preaching (and indeed in all our ministrations) to keep people interested, rivet their attention and make our presentation of the gospel something that at least will get a hearing.

We face two dangers at this point. The first is the danger of oversimplifying the Bible. We must be aware that there are profound issues in the gospel which it is not always easy, or even possible, to make simple. The great doctrines of the trinitarian nature of God, atonement and substitution, election and predestination – even the matter of suffering and evil – are profound things. If we seek to make them too simple we may trivialize them. These truths have their own power, and we must keep them as simple as possible without reducing their overall biblical value.

The second danger is to become impatient with simplicity. While we must guard against being trivial, we must nevertheless remember that God intended the gospel for simple people. We must not become irritated with the inability of people to understand, nor must we become discouraged in trying to help people to understand. Paul tells Timothy to 'correct, rebuke and encourage – with great patience and careful instruction' (2 Tim. 4:2). I can do no better than to close this subsection with a quote from Bishop Ryle:

> Let the best, brightest, and heartiest services be always accompanied by the best and ablest sermons that your minds can produce and your tongues deliver. Let your sermons be addresses in which Christ's blood, mediation, and intercession; Christ's love, power and willingness to save; the real work of the Holy Spirit, repentance, faith, and holiness; are never wanting – sermons full of life, and fire, and power; sermons which set hearers thinking, and make them go home to pray.[12]

Faith

I now move on to discuss the connection of faith with our preaching. This is not often mentioned today, but it needs to be lifted out of obscurity and stressed again. The link between faith and preaching has been explored far more in the writings of bygone days than at present.

Nevertheless it is an element in preaching that needs to be recovered. Do we believe that God will honour his Word?

Horatius Bonar describes the men God used in times of great spiritual awakening. They were, says Bonar, men in great earnest. They were men who dared not be indifferent to the issues; they dared not throw less than their whole soul into the spiritual conflict. But their fervour and zeal were undergirded by faith. 'They ploughed and sowed in hope,' says Bonar.[13] Their tears were tears of sorrow and compassion for their hearers, but not tears of despair. They believed that if they did not faint they would reap in due season; that their labour for Christ would not be in vain. They had confidence in God and his glorious promises; they had confidence in the Holy Spirit's mighty power and grace as the 'quickener' of the soul. They anticipated victory. It was this deep conviction that God would bless their labours that enabled so many of the early preachers and evangelists whose labours and testimonies make up part of our Christian heritage to defy enemies, despise obstacles and persevere in faith.

This great and essential trait is illustrated by Iain Murray in his reference to William Carey's early missionary labours:

> The first evidences of progress – the conversion of Krishna Pal in 1800, and the appearance of Carey's Bengali New Testament in 1801 – were so small as to be unnoticed by the world. But to Carey and his colleagues the Hindu's conversion was momentous. He was only one, but a continent was coming behind him. The divine grace which changed one Indian's heart could obviously change a hundred thousand. Such was their interpretation of the event.[14]

He was expecting a continent to come to Christ. Yet so often we do not expect a congregation to come to Christ. 'These were men', says Bonar, 'who were bent on success. To despair of success would have been a shameful distrust of him who had sent them forth.'[15]

To be sure, sometimes our mission appears discouraging. People may be hard, apathetic, spiritually uninterested and uncaring. It is true that sometimes we see not a flicker of reaction, even after we have preached and pleaded with all our hearts. But we must not give up. We must look and prepare for blessing. If I may be permitted a personal illustration, I have often been invited to churches for an evangelistic service only to arrive and discover that no special preparation has taken place to get unconverted people into the building. No facilities have been made available for anyone who may be spiritually interested. Often after the service the minister has disappeared somewhere to leave me, a stranger, counselling troubled people or enquirers. No helpful literature has been made available. In fact I have learned that sometimes I need to take my own. The very atmosphere is not conducive to any blessing.

What is to account for this state of affairs? There is usually one answer. No-one expects anything to happen. How sad! We must adopt a new mentality. Even if nothing does happen immediately, we must look for it, pray for it, expect it, prepare for it. Our task is impossible, but 'faith laughs at impossibilities' (Charles Wesley). Preachers must be strong in faith, as Charles Haddon Spurgeon recognized:

> To raise the dead is our mission. We are like Peter at Joppa, or Paul at Troas; we have a young Dorcas or Eutychus to bring to life. How is so strange a work to be achieved? If we yield to unbelief we shall be staggered by the evident fact that the work to which the Lord has called us is quite beyond our own personal power. We cannot raise the dead. We are however no more powerless than Elisha, for he could of himself no more restore the Shunnamite son . . . unbelief will whisper to you, 'Can these dry bones live?' But your answer must be, 'O Lord, Thou knowest.'[16]

We must not give up. We must set our hearts on victory. We must anticipate the triumph of the gospel over the hard hearts of men and women. Our preaching must be strengthened and undergirded by faith if the church is to be built.

The power of the Holy Spirit

Let us assume that everything else is in order. We believe and teach the Bible, we have a sense of urgency and an awareness of eternity. We are truly convinced that God will honour his Word. We believe we have been called and equipped for the task, and as far as we can ascertain we walk and live in integrity. What else is lacking? The answer is the power of the Holy Spirit.

I am not referring to the clichés associated with the Pentecostal or charismatic movements. So often this phrase is used to describe phenomena which have nothing whatever to do with gospel purposes or gospel consequences. I am referring rather to that special grace that is given to preachers and teachers to stir the hearts, minds and consciences of their hearers. I am not referring to great entertainers in the pulpit, or to oratory, or to sentimentalism. All these things can move people emotionally. But it is not the mere moving of an audience to tears or laughter that yields eternal results. Rather it is moving an audience toward repentance, faith and holiness. These abilities are not ours. They are God's. Hence the need for the power of the Holy Spirit to accompany our preaching. We need his power to break open hard hearts, to counter the darkness of rebellion and unbelief, to bring spiritual understanding, to grant the new birth, to raise up a determination to persevere in the faith until the end. We preachers need to have this preaching grace, this spiritual strengthening, and power.

Often we feel limp failures after we have preached, only to find it has been a blessing to many; while on other occasions we have felt strong and confident, to discover later that there has been little fruit for our labours. The Holy Spirit works like the wind. He comes and goes as he pleases, but we need him when we preach – not only for preaching purposes, of course, but especially when we are proclaiming God's Word. We must call upon him to pity us in our weakness, to overrule our inadequacies and to grant his blessing. We all know of occasions when our services have been filled with a special sense of his presence. How awe-inspiring yet joyful those occasions are! How we long for those golden moments every time we stand before an audience!

But how are we to obtain his blessing? Apart from humble submission and obedience to God we must resort to prayer. Here we probably fight our greatest spiritual battle, the battle of time and priorities. How easily we become over-busy and burdened! Our minds are filled with a multitude of duties, so that when finally we do sheepishly attempt to seek God's blessing, we fight not only our sense of guilt and failure, but a thousand distractions. We must not exhaust our energies upon external duties and labours and so fail to enrich and fill our own souls with his presence. I know this battle well enough, and often feel that a prayerless week catches up with me five minutes before I preach. We hear again the wise words of Horatius Bonar:

> What might be lost in elaborate composition, or critical exactness of style or argument, would be far more compensated for by the 'double portion of the Spirit' we might then expect to receive.[17]

The words of Edwin Hatch's famous hymn are appropriate here:

> Breathe on me, Breath of God;
> Fill me with life anew,
> That I may love what thou dost love,
> And do what thou wouldst do.
>
> Breathe on me, Breath of God,
> Until my heart is pure,
> Until with thee I will one will,
> To do and to endure.

Breathe on me, Breath of God,
Till I am wholly thine,
Until this earthly part of me
Glows with thy fire divine.

Breathe on me, Breath of God;
So shall I never die,
But live with thee the perfect life
Of thine eternity.

Notes

1. See in this connection the observations of D. Martyn Lloyd-Jones on 'the great pulpiteers' in *Preaching and Preachers* (London: Hodder and Stoughton, new edn. 1971), pp. 13–14.

2. Andrew Bonar, *Memoir and Remains of R. M. M'Cheyne* (Edinburgh: Banner of Truth, 1966), p. 397.

3. *Ibid.*

4. Al Martin, *What's Wrong with Preaching Today?* (Edinburgh: Banner of Truth, n.d.), p. 3.

5. In Andrew Bonar, *op. cit.*, p. 398.

6. In *ibid.*, p. 400.

7. Richard Collier, *The General Next to God* (Glasgow: Collins, 1965), p. 238.

8. J. C. Ryle, *Christian Leaders of the 18th Century* (Edinburgh: Banner of Truth, 1978), p. 204.

9. *Ibid.*, pp. 197f.

10. C. H. Spurgeon, *The Soulwinner* (Pasadena: Pilgrim Publications, 1978), p. 98.

11. Richard Collier, *op. cit.*, p. 242.

12. J. C. Ryle, *No Uncertain Sound* (Edinburgh: Banner of Truth, 1978), pp. 94–95.

13. Horatius Bonar, Introduction to John Gillies, *Historical Collection of Accounts of Revival* (reissue, Edinburgh: Banner of Truth, 1981), pp. vi–vii. The Introduction alone is worth the price of the book.

14. Iain Murray, *The Puritan Hope* (Edinburgh: Banner of Truth, 1971), p. 141.

15. Horatius Bonar, in John Gillies, *op. cit.*, p. vi.

16. C. H. Spurgeon, *op. cit.*, p. 153.

17. Horatius Bonar, in John Gillies, *op. cit.*, p. ix.

9

Preaching that changes the church

Phillip D. Jensen

'Philipp and I drank our beer and the Word did it all.'
(Martin Luther)

It is a great pleasure to contribute this short essay to honour the work of Dick Lucas. God has richly gifted and blessed Dick's preaching, and I consider it a privilege to have had the opportunity to sit under his ministry. Dick's preaching is possibly best described by the oxymoron 'predictably unexpected'.

Its predictability, in terms of consistency with the Word of God and commitment to upholding the gospel of Jesus Christ, is a great hallmark of its authenticity. With such gifts of mind and rhetoric, it would be easy for a man of Dick's ability to give up faithfulness to the message for the kind of speculative novelty that brings worldly honour. But he has stuck persistently to his task and his sermons are predictably biblical.

Yet Dick is unexpected. He always tosses up something of a googly for his hearers. One can never sit counting off the numbers, waiting for him to finish the sermon that one could have preached oneself, because

Dick always wrestles with the Scripture with the freedom of somebody who has confidence in the Author. He is willing to move and to change, to discover and explore the Word of God.

To be predictably unexpected in preaching, such as Dick has demonstrated for years, requires faith in the Word of God. It is Dick's confidence in the truth of God's Word that enables him to value handing on the deposit from one generation to another. It is also his confidence in the Word of God which enables him to explore and mould his life, and the lives of his hearers, by whatever is found there.

Let us commence with four preliminary questions. What church? What change? Why change? Why preaching? After clearing the ground with these preliminary questions, we will turn our attention to the preaching and the preacher that change the church.

What church?

The word 'church' always requires definition. It can refer to our congregations or to denominations or to the worldwide church. Preaching can make the difference at any one of these three levels. The most important level is the local congregation. This is the church of Christ, an expression of the heavenly assembly of all Christ's people gathered together for the wedding of the Lamb.

The state of the gospel in denominations and in the world at large, however, is a sorry mess that needs the change that comes from preaching the Word of God. The establishment and development of the Proclamation Trust and its encouragement to preachers are of enormous importance in developing godly change at the wider level of denominations and community.

What change?

The desire for 'godly change' raises the question of what change to seek. It is because the gospel brings change to a fallen world that Christians should be keen for change: not change from better to worse, however, but from worse to better. So what changes do we desire?

The gospel is a call to repentance. Repentance, by definition, means change. To enter into membership of the church is to undergo that most radical and complete change which humans can ever experience. For true repentance comes from rebirth, the regenerating work of God's Spirit, whose change is a total transformation. Presumably this should happen as we enter the church but, as we know from history, it also happens within the church. We praise God that the work of regeneration and repentance occurs within the lives of church members. It is very sad, however, that members of churches still need regeneration and repentance.

Repentance is but the beginning of the change expected in the life of Christians. Ours must be the long, transforming process of growing like Christ as we put on the robes of righteousness in preparation for the wedding with the Lamb. We must turn to the Lord and be transformed from one degree of glory to another. The Christian who has 'arrived' is already dead and in glory. All other Christians are still in the process of change. The preaching of the Word of God, each week in church, addresses our minds and hearts to keep changing.

Yet the change in the church is not only individual change. For the church itself needs to be built. The building of the church involves both evangelism and the education of the congregation. It is God's sovereign work that gives the growth, through his people planting and watering the field, or, to use another biblical metaphor, laying stones upon the foundations that have already been established. Sometimes the work of change is slow and steady, sometimes quick and dramatic. The moment of repentance can be exactly that: a moment. Yet it can come from the years of Christian education and teaching, as pieces of the truth are slowly laid in the structure of our thinking and as errors are gradually eliminated. The preaching of God's Word will always look to change the church and its members. It will not, however, always be looking for rapid change or be surprised by sudden revolutions.

Changes that happen in the church can differ in ways other than their speed of effect. Some changes are of a radical, first-order character. They involve the transformation of the whole basis of meeting and the way in which we minister to one another. Other changes are of a second-order character, slowly improving and adjusting the character of our fellowship. It is like the difference between becoming a Christian and growing as a Christian. Sometimes we need radically to change the way we conduct church. We need a first-order redirection of the character of our fellowship with one another. Our denominations and the worldwide Christian fellowship are in dire need of such a first-order change. So many of our associations have lost the plot. Sometimes our local congregations also need a radical first-order change, for they too have lost the plot.

Why change?

The above discussion of change explains why we need to change. Evangelism, edification and sanctification all require the church to change. The church is not an organization that is to be described in the phrase 'As it was in the beginning, is now and ever shall be'. The church is a holy temple that is to be built and to grow into Christ, who is our head.

There is another reason preaching should seek to change the church.

The context in which the church is to be built is that of the fallen world. The fallen world not only persecutes the church from outside, but also seduces it and contaminates it from within. We live in the terrible times of the last days when people gather around themselves a great number of teachers to say what their itching ears want to hear, when from within our own number people have arisen to distort the truth and to draw away disciples after themselves, and when the denominations and some congregations have tolerated all manner of Jezebels. This is the context in which we must seek to change the church by preaching the Word of God. That is, we are not trying to change the church in a neutral environment where we have the opportunity to improve and build upon that which has been established. We are trying to change the church in an environment which is working against the proclamation of the gospel, the establishment of the people of God and the growth of the temple of the Lord Jesus Christ. It is precisely because it is such a hostile environment that we must constantly seek to change the church for the better.

Why preaching?

It is fashionable to decry verbal communication and, in particular, preaching. The imperfections and flaws in our capacity to communicate, this side of the tower of Babel, mixed with the problems of epistemology, the 'absolute relativism' of all knowledge, and now the fads and fashions of deconstructionism, have made verbal communication as unfashionable as selling pork on Good Friday in Jerusalem. Add to this our human rebellious, wilful spirit that never wishes to submit to authority or be told what to do, and preaching cannot expect popularity.

God, however, has spoken. He has spoken by prophets and he has now spoken by his Son, who is his Word. Jesus, God's Son, was a preacher. He sent his disciples into the world to preach. We come to new life through the preaching of God's Word. It is the gospel which is the dynamic of God in the world today. For we do not live by bread alone but by every word that proceeds from the mouth of God. It was the Word of God which created the world, flooded the world and will keep the world for the day of judgment. It is the Word of truth that has given us birth: the implanted Word that can save us. For, unlike human beings and their glory, the Word of the Lord stands for ever. It is to this Word that Paul commends the Ephesian elders, for the Word of grace can build and give inheritance among the saints. For the Word of God is not a dead letter but is alive and dynamic, penetrating, dividing and judging. The Word is at work in believers.

Not surprisingly, therefore, the apostles were preachers of the Word of God, and Christ's gifts were the gifts of the Word: apostles, prophets, evangelists, pastors and teachers. What is required of those who speak is that they speak the very words of God. In Paul's instruction of Timothy and Titus about their ministry and their training of others, the teaching of God's Word is paramount. Timothy is to devote himself to the public reading of Scripture, to preaching and to teaching. He is given the solemn charge, before the Judge of all the earth, to preach the Word. He is to entrust to reliable men the things that he has been taught so that they may teach others, and Titus must teach what is in accord with sound doctrine. The church is built on the foundation stone of Jesus Christ, the chief cornerstone, but it is also built on the foundation of the apostles and the prophets. And the elders of the church, who have the solemn responsibility of managing God's household, must have one gift: they must be 'able to teach'.

If the church of Jesus Christ is to be led by God, then it must be led by his Word. His Word is ministered by those leaders and elders of the congregation who conform their lives, and the lives of those for whom they are responsible, to the Word of God. Change in the church comes not by power, or by law, or by economics, or by rules and regulations, or by politics, but by the faithful ministry of the Word of God.

There are other factors involved in changing the church. It is the work of the Spirit, not only in his sword (the Word of God), but also in the hearts of the hearers. It is he who writes on our hearts God's Word and moves us to be obedient to it. And it is not only Timothy's teaching that will save him and his hearers, but also his life lived in conformity to the teaching of the Word of God. Titus is to set an example by doing what is good, as well as by showing integrity and seriousness and soundness of speech in his teaching. And our Father in heaven is responsive to our prayers which come in the name of Jesus. The preaching ministry that would change the church will prayerfully look to the Spirit of God to change the hearts of people so that they may hear, understand and be obedient to the Word of God as the preacher speaks it and exemplifies it in his life. So why preaching? Because it is God's way of working in this world.

Having cleared the undergrowth of these preliminary questions, let us turn to consider the preaching that changes the church and the preacher who will do it. There are two characteristics of this preaching: 'predictability' and 'unexpectedness', and one characteristic of the preacher: faith in the Word of God.

Predictable

The preaching that changes the church must be predictable because it must be faithful to the Word of God. We are not going to change the church for the better by changing the message of the gospel. No amount of demythologization can express the Word of God better than the Scriptures. The message of the gospel is that Jesus Christ is Lord. Central to the lordship of Jesus, the Christ, is that he died for our sins according to the Scriptures, was buried, was raised on the third day, according to the Scriptures, and appeared to Peter and then to the twelve. If those terms are meaningless to people today, then our task is to preach in such a fashion that we can explain the gospel to the people of today. Preachers are not to change the words so that people will understand them, but to change people's understanding so that they will respond to the words.

The gospel is unchangeable. God could not be more explicit in his rejection of changing the gospel. 'Even if we or an angel from heaven should preach a gospel other than the one we preached to you, let him be eternally condemned!' (Gal. 1:8). The gospel that Paul preached in the beginning is the gospel that must be preached in the future. Therefore, the preaching that is going to change the church is predictable.

The gospel can be even spoken of in terms of tradition. 'For what I received I passed on to you' (1 Cor. 15:3). Paul, who was so adamant that he himself was an eyewitness of the risen Christ and received the revelation of the Son of God personally, still passed on the gospel as he had received it. He taught Timothy: 'What you heard from me, keep as the pattern of sound teaching, with faith and love in Christ Jesus. Guard the good deposit that was entrusted to you – guard it with the help of the Holy Spirit who lives in us' (2 Tim. 1:13–14).

The gospel word is not something to discover, improve upon, develop or innovate. The Word of God in Christ Jesus was delivered, once for all, and the faith that we contend for is the faith that was 'once for all entrusted to the saints' (Jude 3). The preaching of the Word of God must be predictable.

This Word of God is written in Scripture. It is not a gospel independent of the Bible, or yet the word found in the Scriptures, but the Scriptures themselves which are the Word of God. It is the exposition of the Bible that is the means of preaching the Word today.

The Scriptures are alive and dynamic and addressed to us. What happened in Moses' generation happened as examples to keep *us* from setting our heart on evil. They were written down as warnings for us 'on whom the fulfilment of the ages has come' (1 Cor. 10:11). 'For everything that was written in the past was written to teach us, so that through endurance and the encouragement of the Scriptures we might have hope' (Rom. 15:4). The Sadducees failed to see that the word of God to Moses at the burning bush was the word of God to the Sadducees in the days of Jesus: 'You are in error because you do not know the Scriptures or the power of God. At the resurrection people will neither marry nor be given in marriage; they will be like the angels in heaven. But about the resurrection of the dead – *have you not read what God said to you*, "I am the God of Abraham, the God of Isaac, and the God of Jacob?"' (Mt. 22:29–32).

It is when we expound the Scriptures as they have been given that our preaching is predictable, as it should be. The agenda of the preaching will not be the agenda of the world but the agenda of the Word. We will not be like so many 'trendoids', scratching the world's itches, following the fashion of ideas and problems, accepting the world's false self-diagnosis and conforming Christian truth to the ever-shifting sands of the weight of scholarly opinions. To minister to any culture, especially our own, requires more than understanding the culture; it requires saying something different. It is the exposition of God's Word that puts us out of step with our culture, and enables us to challenge our culture with the gospel of Jesus. When the church's agenda is set by the issues of the world, then the church is changing from better to worse, for it is being conformed to the world. But when the church's agenda is set by the faithful exposition of God's Word, then the church will be protected from worldliness and will be an open rebuke and challenge to the failures of godless society. This is a change from worse to better.

This faithfulness to the Word of God which produces such predictable preaching also spares us from the tricks and pyrotechnics of rhetoric and enables us to concentrate on the clear, plain statement of the truth. For Paul, the preaching of the word of the cross gave him the wisdom and power of God that human wisdom and debating could never provide. Though his ministry could be seen as weak and unworthy, by confidence in the Word of God, Paul was able to renounce secret and shameful ways, deception and distortion, and set forward the truth plainly (2 Cor. 4:1–3). It means that the faith of believers rests not on man's wisdom but on God's power, and it means that the power to change lives and the church can be seen not to be the preacher's, but God's (1 Cor. 2:4–5).

Thus, church-changing preaching will be predictable preaching. We should be able to go to church each week predicting that God's Word will be expounded, that the preacher will not be off on some new hobby-horse, and that the Lord Jesus will be glorified in the proclamation of his death and resurrection for the salvation of mankind. It is almost the exact reverse of what worldly people expect. They think we will change the church by changing the message, for they do not understand that to change the church from worse to better requires absolute fidelity to the message that was proclaimed in the beginning.

In evangelical circles today, however, everybody 'expounds' the

Scriptures. Oh that it were true! For many so-called expositions of the Scripture are rehearsals of our long-cherished traditions, loosely, even badly and illegitimately, attached to the Scriptures. It is predictable teaching, but it fails to provide the second essential element of the preaching that changes the church, that is, to be unexpected.

Unexpected

Faithful preaching and exposition of the Word of God will, by its very nature, be unexpected. Sinful people, even regenerate Christians, do not think exactly as God thinks. Sometimes our failure to understand God's way of thinking is profound, so profound that we are unconverted. Sometimes, since regeneration, we have come to the mind of Christ, yet our thinking is still distorted by our old nature. Consequently, we always need the Word of God to be changing us. We must not conform that Word to our expectations; rather, we must conform our expectations to that Word.

When we conform the message that we preach to the church's expectations, the Word of God is not being faithfully taught. Certainly, we must be all things to all men so that by all possible means we might save some. Our preaching must never, however, be domesticated to the fads and fashions of society or to church traditions and expectations. The Word of God will keep challenging, rebuking, penetrating, dividing, judging, correcting, training in righteousness and teaching God's people. It is this Word of God, which is living and active, at work in believers, which is the power of God for salvation. This is the dynamic that will change the church.

The Bible not only provides the answers to life's questions; it also provides the questions themselves. So often, when the unbeliever tries to judge Jesus, the Scripture forces him to see that Jesus is judging him. So often, when people come under a faithful exposition of the opening chapters of Genesis, the questions of the twentieth-century mind pale into insignificance, compared to the questions that Genesis raises to the twentieth-century mind. We come as rebellious and wilful people to sit in judgment on the Scriptures, or as Christian people to conform and affirm the views we already hold, only to find the Scriptures sitting in judgment on us and challenging our most deep-seated Christian prejudices. It is not possible to domesticate the Word of God. Therefore, faithful preaching of the Word of God, predictable preaching of the Word of God, will always be unexpected preaching.

The Word of God does not just inform; it also confronts. It is those who *do* the Word of God who understand the Word of God. Parables are not just stories to be told, for they divide the audience into those outside and those inside as they confront the hearers and demand more than casual listening. So preaching that is biblical will always be confrontatory. It may be sweet and gracious, loving and merciful, yet it is a grace that confronts our very fallen nature and understanding.

The message of the Scriptures is not a message of 'balanced Christian living' for the servants of God are called not to be balanced but to be zealous. The preaching of the gospel is similarly zealous. Jesus confronts and challenges, as do the prophets of the Old Testament and as does John the Baptist. Jesus does it with stark contrasts and hyperbole: 'If anyone comes to me and does not hate his father and mother, his wife and children, his brothers and sisters – yes, even his own life – he cannot be my disciple' (Lk. 14:26). Or, 'Sell everything you have and give to the poor, and you will have treasure in heaven. Then come, follow me' (Lk. 18:22). Or, 'Let the dead bury their own dead, but you go and proclaim the kingdom of God' (Lk. 9:60). Jesus' preaching is consistently unexpected and by its very nature ruffles the feathers of those to whom the message is preached.

So it is with the apostles. Paul reminds Timothy: 'You, however, know all about my teaching, my way of life, my purpose, my faith, patience, love, endurance, persecutions, sufferings – what kind of things happened to me in Antioch, Iconium and Lystra, the persecutions I endured. Yet the Lord rescued me from all of them. In fact, anyone who wants to live a godly life in Christ Jesus will be persecuted' (2 Tim. 3:10–12). We would be tempted to change that last word, 'persecuted', to 'rescued'. Paul has been rescued from all his troubles, and we would expect those who live a godly life also to be rescued. But Paul is challenging Timothy to undertake the inevitable persecution that meets those who care to preach the gospel of Jesus Christ. For woe comes to those of whom all men speak well; that is how the false prophets are treated, but blessing rests upon those who are hated and reviled, bad-mouthed and rejected because of Christ and his message. This does not result from balanced, sensible, careful, predictable, affirmation of people's prejudices. This comes from the unexpected nature of the Word of God that challenges people's lives, society and church.

The Christian evangelist is the aroma of Christ: the sweet fragrance of life to those who are being saved, but the stench of death to those who are dying. Nowhere should we expect the opposition to be more fierce than in the religious establishment.

An essential part of confronting the world, especially the world of intellectual relativism, is the capacity to negate. While the Scriptures confirm that everything was made through the Word of God, it is the negation that 'without him nothing was made that has been made' (Jn. 1:3) which really drives home the place of Jesus in creation. He cannot be the first thing created, as the Jehovah's Witnesses wish, for nothing was created without him. It is like the negation, 'I am the LORD, and there is no other' (Is. 45:6), or, 'There is no God apart from me, a righteous God and a Saviour, there is none but me' (Is. 45:21). Monotheism is not the idea that there is one God, but the idea that there is no other God but one God. We cannot adequately teach that the way to God is through Jesus Christ without preaching that no-one comes to the Father except by Jesus. In university missions, very few people complain about the motto 'Know Christ – know life'. But the motto 'No Christ – no life' is always widely despised, because it communicates too clearly. Similarly within the church, be it congregation or denomination, to speak of Christian truths is often acceptable, provided we do not negate heresy and immorality, error and false religion. Yet to be faithful to the Word of God we must denounce idolatry, pouring scorn upon its stupidity and warning against its immorality and blasphemy. We must attack the arrogant folly of taking pride in position, status, robes and titles, all in the name of following the suffering servant whose foot-washing anticipated his execution as the sacrifice for sin. We must 'have nothing to do with the fruitless deeds of darkness, but rather expose them' (Eph. 5:11).

In order to preach the Bible's unexpected message, however, the preacher himself must be surprised by the message. For if the preacher himself does not sit under the Word of God, he cannot bring the church to sit under it either. If the preacher's preparation does nothing more than confirm the preacher's prejudices, then the church will not hear an unexpected sermon. But when the preacher wrestles with the Word of God and finds in it difficulties and seeming obscurities (it is never confusion in the text but always confusion in the preacher), then his sermons come alive with unexpected vitality. Such radicalizing of our own understanding of the Scriptures comes not from superficial preparation, but from deep and prayerful thinking on the meaning of the text itself, with a desperate earnestness to do what it says, and to teach what it says, in its terms, not ours.

The preacher who changes the church

Preaching that is predictable and unexpected comes only from a certain kind of preacher – the preacher who is faithful to the Word of God. All who are evangelicals would want to hold up their hands as those who are faithful to the Word of God. Oh that we all were faithful to the Word of God, and faithful to it all the time!

But faithfulness to the Word of God requires the humility to trust that what God says in his Scripture is more important for the congregation to hear than what the preacher thinks the congregation needs to hear. It requires the humility to trust that explaining the

Scripture, the Scripture's way, will be more valuable in changing lives from worse to better than to answer the questions that are on everybody's lips.

The preacher who is faithful to the Word of God will have certain expectations. He will expect the Word to work powerfully in bringing people to salvation. He will expect it to be at work in believers, changing and transforming them. He will expect it to bring opposition and persecution upon himself. And because he has such confidence in the effective Word of God, he will have the boldness and audacity to stick to the message faithfully.

The preacher who is faithful to the Word of God will also avoid seduction by alternative forms of influence and change. He will not be seduced by the miraculous powers or the words of wisdom of this world, for he will know that it is in the word of the cross that the power of God for salvation and the wisdom of God for salvation are found (1 Cor. 1:24). He will have to be learned in the Word of God, but he will not be seduced by university accreditations and plaudits into preaching the passing fad of 'the assured results of scholarship' in place of the authoritative Word of God. For his authority will not lie in his DMin, but in the truth of the Word that he speaks from God. He will not be tempted by the power of the institutional church, or seduced by wealth, title and personal advancement, to domesticate or sanitize the Word. Any preacher who would ever wish to change the church must undergo one fundamental change of heart: he must destroy any desire or ambition for personal advancement or acceptance within congregation or denomination, especially that rationalized ambition 'that when I come to power I will be able to change things for the better'. As long as a man desires to be a bishop or a moderator, he will not be a faithful preacher of the Word of God, or a preacher who will change the church from worse to better.

It is the fear of God with which Paul challenges Timothy to the ministry of preaching the Word: 'In the presence of God and of Christ Jesus, who will judge the living and the dead, and in view of his appearing and his kingdom, I give you this charge: Preach the Word' (2 Tim. 4:1–2). We are not answerable to one another, or to the congregation, or even to ourselves, but to God. It is why tenure in some form is so important to faithful preaching of the gospel. The preacher who is under the authority and financial control of the denomination or of the congregation will be severely hampered in preaching the predictably unexpected message of God. It is why preachers must be willing to risk all, even sacking and imprisonment, if they are going to be faithful to preaching the gospel.

To be preachers who change the church requires us to be preachers who have faith in the sufficiency of the Scriptures. It is only confidence that the Scriptures will do God's work that will enable a preacher to preach the Word predictably and unexpectedly; that is, to preach in a way which will change the church from worse to better.

10

Preaching that understands the world

D. A. Carson

I am grateful that the title of this chapter is not 'Preaching that Attempts to be Relevant'. To put the subject that way tends, in our culture of the immediate, to raise 'relevance' beyond its proper pragmatic importance to the place where it exercises a controlling veto; if something in a sermon is not perceived to be relevant, it must be excised. Part of the problem with such an approach is that 'relevance' is often confused with 'what is perceived to be relevant'. After all, something may be extremely relevant but not be perceived to be so by many people. On the other hand, if some truths in a sermon are by biblical and theological standards extremely relevant to those who are listening even while those who are listening doubt their relevance, it is the preacher's responsibility to help the hearers see and feel the relevance, and thus diminish the gap between relevance and perceived relevance.

Clearly the 'relevance' category may quickly become very confusing. But if there are dangers lurking for preachers who try so hard to be relevant that they soon degenerate to the trendy, the cutesy, and the shockingly unbiblical, other dangers lie in wait for preachers who think they are above such matters. They simply want to be 'biblical'; they are going to spoon out the truth in dollops of firm propositions, honourably and boldly, without garnish.

The sad truth of the matter is that often these offenders are graduates of our better seminaries and theological colleges. There they have devoted countless hours to mastering the rudiments of responsible exegesis and informed theological reflection, but most of them have thought little about culture. Fellow students in the missions department will take courses on cross-cultural communication, and thus be forced to wrestle with what it means to understand and to communicate with a world other than their own. But many a preacher has given little thought to such matters, and therefore lines up with the principal offenders.

The challenge is becoming more urgent as western cultures change and diversify so quickly. Preachers may think they are addressing their own culture because, after all, this is where they were brought up, these are the people they know – all the while failing to recognize that they have retreated into a much smaller Christian subculture largely at odds with the surrounding oceans of culture. Not only the rapidity of the change but also the diversity of what is on offer in even one small country multiplies the hurdles. In America, graduates of the institution where I teach will be called upon to preach the gospel and plant churches in Tulsa, Oklahoma, where they may find it difficult to find many people who will admit to not being a Christian, and in New England towns with prestigious universities, where the majority of students are utterly biblically illiterate and simultaneously convinced that Christianity is to be dismissed as one form of religious bigotry. In the United Kingdom, preachers are called upon to proclaim the whole counsel of God in run-down parts of East London, in Oxford and in other university towns, in traditional churches in Suffolk, in posh areas of Sussex, to blue-collar workers in industrial centres, in towns once renowned for coal-mining but now primarily characterized by un-employment and sullen resentments, in Scottish cities that combine the most remarkable mix of noble theological heritage and committed secularism, in the Principality of Wales where nationalism inevitably plays some part in all cultural values, in racially mixed Leicester, and in Ulster where 'the Troubles' still constitute a backdrop one can never quite ignore. The sheer diversity is staggering.

The sermon is not an art form to be admired. 'Preaching *is not* speaking *about* truth *before* the congregation, but rather *speaking truth to the congregation*.'[1] That means we can never afford to be careless about how well what we say is understood. Stephen Neill is not far off the mark with this metaphor: 'Preaching is like weaving. There are the two factors of the warp and the woof. There is the fixed, unalterable element, which for us is the Word of God, and there is the variable element, which enables the weaver to change and vary the pattern at his will. For us that variable element is the constantly changing pattern of people and of situations.'[2] What, then, are some of the elements that preachers need to bear in mind as they wrestle with this component of their task? I shall mention five things.

1. The primacy of a biblical understanding of the world

The importance of this point cannot be too greatly stressed. The Bible demands that we look at the world, that we understand it, in certain ways. We shall shortly see that this leaves plenty of scope for sensitivity to an assortment of variable features, but this first element is foundational to the preacher's task.

The place we must begin in our attempt to understand the world from the Bible's perspective is with the large-scale features in the Bible's plot-line. To clarify this point, three comments may be useful.

1. By 'plot-line' or 'story-line' I am not suggesting that the Bible's developing 'story' should be compared with the developing 'story' of, say, a nineteenth-century novel (*i.e.* a work of fiction). Rather, I am merely pointing out that, in addition to a rich plethora of psalms, wisdom sayings, laments, oracles, proverbs, discourses, apocalyptic descriptions, and other genres, the Bible as a whole provides a coherent narrative account. It tells a story, the plot unfolding from creation to consummated new creation.

2. By 'large-scale features' in the Bible's plot-line, I am referring to those elements of such importance that they are picked up again and again by later biblical writers, and without which the Bible's 'story' loses its coherence. For example, one may quibble about the precise canonical contribution of, say, Micaiah's prophecy (as important as it is for certain topics; 1 Ki. 22; 2 Ch. 18), but one must not duck the strategic contribution of the fall (Gn. 3). To put the matter another way, one could comfortably summarize the Bible's story-line in half an hour, and choose to omit the account of Micaiah, not because it is unimportant for all purposes but because the main contours of the Bible's plot-line would not lose their coherence if the Micaiah account were not included. But one could not responsibly summarize the Bible's plot-line in half an hour and omit the fall. To lose the fall, and all the biblical reflection that flows from it (*e.g.* Rom. 1:18 – 3:20), would be to lose what is wrong with the human race, and therefore the necessary background to what salvation consists in, and how it is achieved.

3. Obviously this sort of approach presupposes that the Bible does in

fact embrace a coherent story-line. For those who think that the Bible contains no more than an interesting mixture of religious experiences, some of which are mutually incompatible, there is little point in trying to discern a coherent plot-line. Discussion must begin farther back, with the nature of revelation, with the nature of the personal/ transcendent God who talks and discloses himself. For those who think that the Bible should be read primarily as a handbook of case studies,[3] there will be little attempt to integrate its various parts along the backbone of its story-line. At issue, then, is not only the Bible's authority, but how it is to be read.

There is no space here to justify the primacy of reading the Bible as a unified book with a coherent story-line. I am merely affirming such primacy, insisting that the way we understand the world must be decisively shaped by the theology that emerges from the development of the Bible's plot-line.

An example may bring this point into focus. The western world has gone through successive waves of the nature/nurture debate. Are people primarily determined in their conduct by their nature (now commonly tied to genetics) or by the ways in which they were brought up, shaped by family and surrounding subculture? As long as the Freudian model was regnant, appeal was commonly made to human *nature* as pre-eminently sexual, and to human *nurture* in terms of childhood and later experiences of sexuality. The rise of behaviourism, whether the fairly ruthless form of B. F. Skinner or something more moderated, plus the influence of cultural anthropologists such as Margaret Mead, heavily emphasized the 'nurture' side: behaviour is culturally determined. During the last decade and a half, however, the mushrooming developments in the field of genetics have increasingly tilted the argument towards 'nature'. Scientists have tried to discover statistical alignments between many kinds of behaviour and peculiar genes or neural structures.

In neither model does the nature of sin as an offence against the personal/transcendent God who made us feature prominently. Biblically faithful Christianity leaves place for cultural influence: the sins of the fathers are visited on the children (ask anyone who has dealt with sexual abuse), and the sowing of the wind issues in the reaping of the whirlwind. Similarly, biblically faithful Christianity leaves place for genetics, even for flawed genes: we are body/spirit beings, not mere shells for vitalism, and the curse we have attracted means that our bodies, like our spirits, break down in complex and horrible ways. But at its heart, Christianity will always want to insist that what makes sin evil is its defiance of the Creator God; that the thing to fear most about sin is not the social consequences, as awful as they may be, but the certain judgment of God ('fear him who can destroy body and soul in hell', Mt. 10:29); that what we need most is reconciliation to this God; that God himself has provided this reconciliation in the death and resurrection of his Son; and much more along the same lines.

In other words, the Christian charge is that most contemporary analyses of the human dilemma are shallow and reductionistic, because they do not take into account the real nature of sin and of objective guilt. The human dilemma, understood in modern secular categories, can be repaired by judicious social tinkering, psychological insight and counselling, guilt-free self-understanding, humanistic education, and a great deal of government money. Not for a moment do I think that nothing good can come of such ventures. But they are, finally, too shallow; they are not sufficiently radical, they do not go to the *radix*, the root, of the problem. They do not deal with the real guilt we incur before God; they do not take seriously enough the nature of evil and its effects.

Far from being a detour, this somewhat abstract discussion is critical for preachers who want to understand the world. We will not be seduced by the trendy visions of the world that come and go, if we have already adopted without reservation what the Bible has to say about the fall and about sin. In this century we have at various points been told that education and largesse would reform all the world and bring it into line with 'civilized' humanism; that the First World War was the war to end all wars; that with the decline of totalitarian Marxism we are entering a new order of relative peace; that we can trust the wisdom and goodness of the American (or British or Canadian or whatever) people. We seem to forget that the founders of the American republic (to go no further) were nervous about too much democracy, precisely because they believed in the propensity of human beings to be selfish and evil. That is why they established a system of checks and balances: never let any one group enjoy too much unchecked power. At the personal level, we are regularly told, explicitly or implicitly, that our problems are invariably societal and not personal; that self-fulfilment is the highest good; that the person who acquires the most wins.

Into this construction of reality strides the preacher who believes what the Bible says about sin. He believes that it is honourable to strive for peace, but he holds that until Jesus returns there will be wars and rumours of wars: he is not seduced by 'new order' speeches or announcements that we have just fought the war to end wars. Although he values a good education, he recognizes that educated sinners are still sinners, possibly very clever sinners. With Churchill, he believes that democracy is the worst form of government, except for all the others – that is, he does not think of democracy as being strong or right or fair because of the essential goodness of the citizens and of their corporate judgment, but because it seems like the best way to limit any one group from becoming so powerful that evil becomes formidably institutional-ized. While trying to understand the complex nature of sin, never does he minimize personal responsibility. The suggestion that self-fulfilment is the *summum bonum* he dismisses as idolatrous twaddle: he remembers that Jesus taught that only those who deny themselves, take up their cross and follow him find life.

This means that the Christian preacher will never look at the world exactly the way non-Christians will. Moreover, this one area, how one thinks about sin, is interlocked with so many others. One remembers the biting words of the poetess Phyllis McGinley, describing her creation, the Reverend Doctor Harcourt:

> And in the pulpit eloquently speaks
> On divers matters with both wit and clarity:
> Art, Education, God, the Early Greeks,
> Psychiatry, Saint Paul, true Christian charity,
> Vestry repairs that must shortly begin –
> All things but Sin. He seldom mentions Sin.[4]

And if there is no mention of sin, what need of a Saviour? If sin is transmuted to social disorder or personal want of integration, what need for reconciliation with the God who made us? Worse, if we *think* there is no odious sin, no objective guilt, no judgment to be averted, *while these realities continue unrecognized*, not only do we entertain massively distorted visions of the world, but we are in the utmost danger.

In these last few paragraphs I have been describing one small but crucial element in the Bible's plot-line which, if believed, shapes the preacher's understanding of the world. But there are many others. Creation establishes the relation between creature and Creator; what the Bible says about being made in the image of God demands that we think of human beings in certain ways and not in others; the judgment of the flood illuminates what God thinks of our rebellion, and anticipates the judgment still to come; and so forth. A profound grasp of the Bible's story-line from creation to the new heaven and the new earth must not be viewed as useful information that nicely explains the nature of personal salvation, and nothing more. It provides an *essential* way of looking at the world. *It is impossible to remain faithful to the apostolic gospel unless we remain faithful to the biblical understanding of the world.*

2. The importance of understanding a particular culture

Notwithstanding what I have said about the critical importance of a fundamentally biblical understanding of the world, it is essential for preachers to integrate with their general Christian understanding of the world an acute and accurate understanding of the particular culture where they minister. I shall restrict myself to six comments.

1. Cultures differ from one another.[5] The construals of reality in the pantheistic branches of Hinduism, in the frankly atheistic strands of Buddhism, in the rising secularization characteristic of modern Deism, and in a providential view of history that is tied to robust theism, are all very different. On a much smaller scale, socially formed values vary enormously: one's sense of humour, the role of the extended family, one's view of the importance of time, the value placed on the tribe or the nation, the level of education, acceptable forms of social interaction, and much more. I have not mentioned differences in language, and of course every language is a cultural phenomenon. An Australian aboriginal will not meet your gaze, because he is being polite and treating you with respect, and you think him shifty-eyed. An American tourist in Europe talks loudly of his possessions and accomplishments, and we think him arrogant and boorish, while he thinks of himself as frank, open, candid. An Englishman visits Rio and his reserve is interpreted as haughtiness and coldness. Cultures are different.

2. Although cultures must be learned if competent communication is to take place, for most preachers such learning is simply part of their own enculturation. In other words, where a preacher really has been part of his own culture, and has reflected deeply upon it, he may be able to address it quite easily without ever formally studying it. If he is among his own people, he is in a situation quite different from that of the cross-cultural preacher.

That is one of the reasons some preachers prove largely unacceptable in cultures outside their own. I know a preacher with a dismal record in New England who proved remarkably fruitful in California – and the difference in fruitfulness was not to be explained purely on the grounds of different receptivity of the soils, for some preachers are fruitful in New England. A preacher in old England may prove singularly unsuitable in Wales – and *vice versa* – even when there is scarcely a scrap of theological difference between the two. Other preachers are more transportable: one thinks, for instance, of the wide-scale influence of a Lloyd-Jones. In many instances there is peculiar unction on their lives. But part of the issue lies in the fact that such preachers are not so narrowly tied to their home culture that they seem idiosyncratic and even odd to others.

Moreover, if someone is asked to speak in another culture, it is often the mark of courtesy and love to learn something of that culture. This is the more urgent where the sermons are to be preached to unbelievers. A largely Christian congregation may make more allowances than a non-Christian audience. When I have first gone to a country that is new to me, and where at least part of my assignment has been to preach evangelistically, I have almost always perused at least half a dozen or a dozen books on that country's history, social matrix, values, customs, heritage, and so forth, as part of my preparation.

3. Cultures change. They are not static. Implicitly we recognize this when we hear elderly people reminisce about the good old days. Very often a substantial component of what they are saying is that the culture they had thought of as their own has so changed that they now feel alien and isolated. Owing to a number of factors, cultures in the western world are changing at an accelerating pace. In addition, most western countries now boast far more empirical pluralism than they did a generation ago. This makes the challenge of reaching out with the gospel to these new subcultures more of what has traditionally been thought of as a missionary enterprise – *i.e.* in some measure it demands the skills of cross-cultural communication. We work at such matters when we go to a foreign land; for some of us, it is harder to work at them when they are demanded in the land of our birth.

4. Understanding a particular culture is not exactly the same thing as taking on board what the people of that culture think of themselves. Nor is it exactly the same thing as reading the latest sociology reports analysing that culture. We must of course grasp what people think of themselves, and we do well to understand social trends. But at this point my first and second headings meet: while trying to understand a culture, we must still be trying to think biblically and theologically.

This means we shall be obliged to decide what cultural elements are largely neutral, what are to be opposed and reformed by the gospel, what are the fruit of common grace and therefore to be espoused and cherished. Latin Americans like to reduce the distance between two people to about eighteen inches; Anglos are more comfortable with about a yard. To Anglos, Latins are pushy; to Latins, Anglos are aloof and cold. There is nothing moral or divinely sanctioned about thirty-six inches as opposed to eighteen. The preacher of the gospel learns to flex, learns the communication signals endemic to the culture. But when he confronts, say, the cargo cults that flourish in the Melanesian islands, sooner or later he must challenge them, expose the underlying covetousness (often unwittingly fostered by expatriates) as idolatry, and seek to bring men and women to a better treasure. Doubtless it is helpful to learn the characteristic outlooks of baby-boomers and baby-busters, but the preacher will also want to think through what characteristics of, say, baby-busters, are so drenched in myopic self-ishness that repentance and reformation are called for. And if for reasons of communication a preacher *begins* with the self-perceived interests and needs of his people, sooner or later he must establish links between these and the Bible's agenda, or he should stay out of the pulpit.

5. The purpose of such growing understanding of the culture in which God has placed the preacher is not only to praise God for the diversity of gifts and peoples he has placed upon the earth (however much they are corroded by sin), but to learn better how to communicate the gospel to the peoples of these diverse cultures.

This can usefully be seen as a two-step process. The student of Scripture must try to understand the Bible on its own terms, within the cultures in which it was first given, and then learn to transport and apply its truth into his or her own world. The Bible is not an abstract manual, stripped of all cultural elements: to his glory, God has disclosed himself to real men and women, and ultimately in a real Man – and that necessarily means at peculiar times and places and in peculiar cultures and languages. Faithful biblical exegesis demands sufficient hermeneutical awareness that we recognize the difficulties of understanding a text that is two thousand and more years old, and written in languages not our own. We seek the Spirit's help, while recognizing that the burden of responsibility falls upon us as we wrestle with the responsibility and privilege of interpretation. Thus we traverse the cultural barriers that separate biblical times from our own. But then in our tasks as preachers, we may have to cross another cultural barrier – the one to our audiences. For most preachers in the western world, this does not involve a language barrier, but there may be several others. Our hearers may be biblically illiterate, or steeped in New Age categories, or entirely out of sympathy with biblical absolutes, or swamped by vague notions of spirituality that drown the biblical message in sentimentalism. Now our task is to articulate the message of Scripture across these new cultural barriers. We seek the Spirit's help, while recognizing that the burden of responsibility and privilege in heralding the gospel accurately and comprehensibly falls on us.

As western culture progressively drifts away from its Judeo-Christian heritage, new challenges to accurate and forceful communication are erected. It is sometimes helpful to think in terms of 'plausibility structures'. A plausibility structure is a social structure of ideas that is widely taken for granted without argument, and dissent from which is regarded as heresy. For a long time the plausibility structures of our culture were in large measure Christian. It was widely accepted, without debate, that there was a difference between right and wrong and between truth and error; that human beings have been made by God and for God, who will one day be our Judge; that God sets the rules; that he sent his son Jesus. Even if people were a little fuzzy as to who Jesus was or what he did, these were among the 'givens'. Today, however, as empirical pluralism develops, there are fewer and fewer plausibility structures in most western nations, but the ones that remain are tenaciously held. And these are anything but Christian: no religion is superior to any other religion; God exists primarily for my satisfaction and fulfilment; God is so much a God of love it is unthinkable that he could be angry; all religions say much the same thing anyway; religion is not a matter of objective truth but of subjective faith.

The changes in western plausibility structures mean that the task of the preacher to communicate the faith 'once delivered to the saints' is becoming more challenging. Understanding the world in which we live is a first step; the faithful proclamation of the gospel is the primary motivation.

6. In some measure these perspectives are already mirrored in the pages of the New Testament. In Luke's witness, Paul does not approach people in the synagogue in Pisidian Antioch in exactly the same way that he approaches people in pagan Athens. This is not because his gospel changes; it is because his audience has changed. In the context of the synagogue, Paul assumes that his hearers are more or less biblically literate, and have adopted plausibility structures in line with the old-covenant Scriptures. He therefore seeks to persuade them that Jesus fulfils the promises that God made in those Scriptures. In Athens, where most of his hearers would not so much as have heard of the Bible, much less read it, and where the plausibility structures were shaped by one branch or another of Greek paganism, Paul had to begin farther back – with the personal/transcendent God, God's aseity, the doctrine of creation, the ground of human responsibility, the prospect of judgment, divine providence, teleology in history, and more – before he even introduces Jesus Christ. The reason, of course, is that if he had introduced Jesus first, all that he said about him would have been misunderstood. The worldview had to change; the plausibility structures had to change. And Paul, gifted preacher that he was, understood such matters, and shaped his preaching accordingly.

3. The challenge of understanding a particular culture

The difficulties are many; I mention only a few.

1. Many Christians in the western world, including Christian preachers, feel betrayed. The Judeo-Christian heritage they called their own has, they feel, come unstuck, and those who are responsible are the · enemy. If you want to sell a book in the Christian press today, one sure way of doing it is to write a volume of pure negativism – all the things that are wrong in education, politics, bioethics, marriages, child-rearing, values, or whatever. God knows there is enough around us to criticize. But one wonders if some of the popularity of such books stems not from their prophetic stance, but from the fact that many people feel fed

up and betrayed by the changes, and these books allow them to vent their spleen vicariously. Seldom do these books point the way forward; they simply keep our disgust fresh. Preachers may buy into such negativism, adopting a 'them *versus* us' stance that is so strong there are almost no incentives for genuinely understanding what the world is saying.

2. As western culture is progressively de-Christianized,[6] Christians tend to regroup into holy huddles. Their friends are Christians, and in these Christian crowds there is a kind of sanctified discourse that excludes outsiders. If Christians, not least Christian preachers, spend all their time in such circles, it becomes harder and harder to communicate effectively with unbelievers.

For this reason preachers need to seek out unbelievers, hostile audiences, evangelistic opportunities. They need to do so not only because those who hear need to listen to the gospel, but because they themselves need to study the minds of unbelievers if they are going to proclaim the gospel to the people of the prevailing culture, and not only to those of the confessing church.

3. The sheer speed of the changes proves daunting for some. A preacher who exercised fruitful ministry among university students twenty-five years ago may find a university crowd distinctly alien today, if he has not laboured in that environment in the interval. In that period we have moved from modernism to postmodernism, from Marxist rhetoric to radical feminism, from the new criticism to deconstruction, from scepticism about religion to radical philosophical pluralism. Similar changes have afflicted the larger culture, though not quite so quickly or extensively.

4. Some of us, quite frankly, are short of compassion, of Christ-like love. We see the evils, and we denounce them – quite rightly; but we lack the response of Jesus, who, looking on crowds of men and women, sees sheep without a shepherd, and is moved with compassion. Jesus denounces, but he weeps over the city. Where such love is operative, it will find a way to understand the culture, so as to be able the better to apply the whole counsel of God to as many people as possible. Practically speaking, this means time and energy devoted to an empathetic understanding of the people to whom the Lord has sent us, to an imaginative grasp of how their lives appear to them.

4. Some large-scale cultural elements in the western world

I have hinted at some of these; elsewhere I have discussed them at length.[7] It is enough here to mention a handful, more by way of example than as a responsible representation.

1. On the whole, the intellectual world in the West has shifted from modernism to postmodernism. The former period (roughly 1600–1970) was characterized by brimming confidence in human reason to uncover absolute truth, by rising commitment to philosophical naturalism, to nice distinctions between the 'facts' of science and the opinions of 'faith'. Postmodernity, having bought into one form or another of radical hermeneutics, holds that all 'knowledge' is either a personal or a social construct, is never absolute, and is conditioned by just about everything (language, heritage, presuppositions, what side of the bed you got out of this morning). The only heresy left is the heresy that there is such a thing as heresy. Modernism had its critics, of course, and so now does postmodernism. Thoughtful Christians will not want to buy into either package, while still recognizing some valid points in both worldviews. But they do see the change that has come about. It is exemplified in the way people respond to, say, a sermon with a firm argument for the resurrection of Jesus. Three decades ago, such a sermon might have provoked an argument about the evidence; today, one is far more likely to hear, 'I'm so glad you have found your faith helpful to you. But what about all the Muslims who don't believe that Jesus rose from the dead?'

Especially those preachers who minister to university students must devote some thought to the challenges of postmodernity, including deconstruction, radical pluralism, shifting positions on the nature of 'truth', and revised epistemologies.

2. Rising biblical illiteracy means that fewer and fewer people have many mental 'pegs' on which to hang what you say. This means that responsible biblical preaching must spend more time recounting the basic biblical story-line and its principal theological lesson – not unlike Paul in Athens in Acts 17. In evangelistic work today I assume that people do not know that the Bible has two Testaments, that for them 'sin' is a naughty snicker-word without a trace of real odium, that 'God' is a plastic word with who knows what content, and so forth.

3. With the dilution of the Judeo-Christian heritage, fewer and fewer people feel shame when they sin. That means that responsible preaching must not only proclaim the gospel but explicate the need for the gospel – and that means a return to the doctrine of God, the nature of law, the inevitability of judgment, along with the wonders of grace. At the same time, most preachers with long memories are facing far more broken homes, abused women, children of alcoholic parents, emotional teenagers in adult bodies, than they did twenty-five years ago. That spells a need for expository preaching on how to live. Paul is concerned that his readers remember not only his doctrine, but his way of life; our concern must be no narrower.

4. Intoxicated by the media, more and more people think they have

the right to be entertained. They never have to think; they are never alone, since they can always switch on the television or the CD-player or the home computer. Some Christian leaders simply denounce the trend; others try to make the 'worship experience' more entertaining (not least the sermon), and thus provide a little competition.

This is one of the most sensitive issues in churches in the western world. Certainly there is no intrinsic merit in being boring; on the other hand, the liveliness generated by excitement is not necessarily a sign of spiritual vitality. On the long haul, the way forward is, on the one hand, to understand the diversity of cultural expressions of genuine worship and praise, and, on the other, to insist that services and sermons bend constantly toward the goal of glorifying God and knowing and enjoying him, by God's grace generating a people who refuse to be squeezed into the world's mould.

5. Modern fuzzy notions of 'spirituality' demand clarity of thought and proclamation about what is truly 'spiritual' in the light of Christ's cross-work and of the Spirit whom he bequeathed.

6. The pressures on our schedules, derived from many expectations imposed by ourselves or others, strip us of the time and energy needed to read, think, meditate, study, pray. This is the stuff of all vital preaching. Where it is slashed back, whatever time remains for sermon preparation tends to get shoved into one task: understanding the text. Certainly that is a necessary task, but it is not the only one. We must devote adequate time to understanding the world in which God has placed us, if we are to minister tellingly to the men and women to whom God has sent us.

5. Some practical suggestions

1. Most preachers ought to devote more time to reading, to reading widely. It is never right to skimp in Bible study, theology, church history, or excellent biography; but in addition, we must read books and journals and news magazines that help us understand our own age and culture. In his book on preaching, John Stott provides a list of titles he has found helpful.[8] The list is now a little dated. Without here taking the space to provide my own list, perhaps I may mention several of the principles that govern my own reading (outside Scripture, comment-aries, theology, *etc.*). First, I try to read material from competing perspectives. I may subscribe for two or three years to the left-of-centre *New York Review of Books* and *Sojourners*, and then cancel the subscriptions and subscribe for a while to right-of-centre *Chronicles*. Secondly, certain authors I regularly skim: Os Guinness, George Marsden, Thomas Sowell, James Davison Hunter, Peter Berger, and others – not because I agree with all they say, but because they are

trying to understand the culture. Thirdly, occasionally I read 'blockbuster' books, simply because so many people are reading them that I think I must find out what is shaping the minds of many fellow citizens. Fourthly, occasionally I devote a block of time – six months, say, or a year – to try to get inside some new movement. For instance, I devoted a considerable block to reading the primary authors in the various schools of deconstruction. Fifthly, I have sometimes subscribed for a period of time to a first-class literary journal such as *Granta*. Sixthly, I occasionally subscribe to reports from the reputable pollsters, to discover drifts and trends in the nation – Gallup, Yankelovich, and others.

Not everyone reads at the same rate; not everyone's ministry requires the same extent of reading. Some manage far more than I. At no time should such reading ever squeeze out the primary importance of understanding the Word of God. But selective rapid reading of many sources can help preachers better understand the world in which they serve.

2. Discussion with friends and colleagues with similar interests is a great help. This may be formal, for instance an agreed evening once a month to discuss book X or film Y in the light of Christian commitments; it may be informal, depending, of course, on the structures and friendships of one's life. No-one understands everything; thoughtful, widely read and devout friends are to be cherished and nourished.

3. Nowadays there are some good tapes. I sometimes drive substantial distances, but never without tapes. The *Mars Hill Tapes* offer good value for money. In addition, many ministries today are recorded, and preachers do well to listen to other preachers who are particularly gifted in the handling of the Word and in applying it to life.

4. It is essential to talk with non-Christians, whether one on one, in small groups, or to large crowds. There is no more important avenue toward understanding our world.

And when all is done, return again to Scripture, and remember my first point.

Notes

1. John Bettler, 'Application', in Samuel T. Logan Jr (ed.), *The Preacher and Preaching: Reviving the Art in the Twentieth Century* (Welwyn: Evangelical Press, 1986), p. 333 (emphasis his).

2. Stephen Neill, *On the Ministry* (London: SCM, 1952), p. 74.

3. *E.g.* Charles Kraft, *Christianity in Culture: Dynamic Biblical Theologizing in Cross-Cultural Perspective* (Maryknoll: Orbis, 1980).

4. Phyllis McGinley, *Times Three* (New York: Viking, 1961), pp. 134–135.

5. The term 'culture' is notoriously difficult to define. This is typical: 'It is that entire body of received information: ideas, opinions, attitudes, values, beliefs, and experiences that constitute a particular social and historical moment or epoch and are appropriated by an individual and community as the common life of humanity within prescribed boundaries' (so John S. McClure, *The Four Codes of Preaching*, Minneapolis: Fortress, 1991, p. 136). Perhaps this definition is too narrowly conceptual, insufficiently behavioural and relational; certainly culture includes not less than what is stated here.

6. I am aware of statistics that say that in some western countries (*e.g.* the US) the number of people who say they go to church at least once a month has been stable, within about 15%, for a century. But such statistics are misleading. Some researchers have questioned whether or not people are doing what they say they are doing (how many check to see if people really do go to church?). More importantly, the pressures of secularization squeeze religion to the periphery, so that mere church-attendance figures say little about the importance of religion in the life of an individual or in the life of the nation.

7. See D. A. Carson, *The Gagging of God: Christianity Confronts Pluralism* (Grand Rapids: Zondervan, 1995).

8. John R. W. Stott, *I Believe in Preaching* (London: Hodder and Stoughton, 1982), pp. 194ff.

11

Preaching that converts the world

John Chapman

When the apostle Paul says, 'I am not ashamed of the gospel' (Rom. 1:16), we cannot take seriously the idea that he was. Perhaps his tongue was in his cheek. Whoever would have believed that he was ashamed of it? He had endured great hardship for the sake of the gospel (2 Cor. 11:23–29). There was no doubt in anyone's mind. He was not ashamed of it. In fact, he had been its champion from the day he was arrested by the risen Lord Jesus on the road to Damascus (Acts 26:12–23). He was commissioned there to be the apostle to the Gentiles with the explicit instruction, 'I am sending you to them to open their eyes and turn them from darkness to light, and from the power of Satan to God, so that they may receive forgiveness of sins and a place among those who are sanctified by faith in me' (Acts 26:17–18). Paul was obedient to that heavenly vision, and he had seen the fruit of his labours in the form of new churches planted wherever he preached.

He had good cause not to be ashamed of it because he had witnessed at first hand that 'it is the power of God for the salvation of everyone who believes' (Rom. 1:16).

We live in an age when Christian people crave for power from God. It is, however, with sadness that so many seem to have missed this God-given method of attaining it. In the gospel lies the power of God to save those who believe. On any Sunday, for those with eyes to see, the power of the gospel is evident at churches all over the world, in men and women whose lives have been transformed by the power of the gospel. Often these people have nothing in common except faith in Christ, and yet this binds them into a fellowship which can rightly be described as the body of Christ. This happened through the gospel. The gospel has changed them. *It is a very powerful message.*

It has done this not only throughout the world, but also throughout the course of history. People from diverse backgrounds, different cultures, different ethnic groupings, have all been transformed by the message that 'God was reconciling the world to himself in Christ' (2 Cor. 5:19). When John is shown a vision of heaven, he says, 'I looked and there before me was a great multitude that no-one could count, from every nation, tribe, people and language, standing before the throne and in front of the Lamb' (Rev. 7:9). How did they get there? They had 'washed their robes and made them white in the blood of the Lamb' (Rev. 7:14). They had put their trust in the saving death of the Lord Jesus! It was through the powerful message of the gospel.

On a Sunday in January 1994 the truth of this was brought home to me powerfully. I had been invited to preach at the Vietnamese Church at Cabramatta, a suburb of Sydney. We met at 3.45pm. It was cold outside and inside. The congregation was small by Australian standards. The service was conducted in Vietnamese, of which I am completely ignorant. The pastor's wife interpreted for me. Those who have been interpreted know how difficult it is. I spoke; she interpreted; I spoke again. It was nearly impossible to create any atmosphere, even if we wanted to. I preached on the parable of the Pharisee and the tax-collector. At the conclusion of the sermon I prayed for people to receive Christ, and sat down. What the pastor said I did not understand, but he phoned me later and said that he had asked people who had received Christ to tell him, so that he could organize some follow-up for them. He told me that several people had spoken to him and said that they had responded to the gospel.

It is amazing. Those people and I had almost nothing in common. They were refugees and had terrible stories to tell. I have lived a sheltered life. We were culturally poles apart. Most of them could not understand my English, and I could hardly follow theirs. We were both part of humankind and we both lived in Australia; that seemed to be the extent of our common ground. When preaching was taking place, there were long pauses between what was said. Sometimes the interpreter did not understand an illustration, or some part of the sermon, and still people heard the voice of God, were arrested and turned back to the true and living God.

We also have nothing to be ashamed of. The gospel *is* the power of God to save those who believe.

If gospel preaching is depreciated, we cut ourselves off from the God-ordained way of bringing people to salvation. Rather than being some optional extra, the gospel is at the heart of Christian ministry. Certainly the apostle to the Gentiles believed this (Acts 20:20). Those ministers who faithfully preach the gospel Sunday by Sunday know that this is so. Evangelistic preaching is not to be thought of as preaching by special evangelists, but as the regular preaching ministry of all pastors.

Several years ago I was conducting a series of evangelistic meetings in the St George area of Sydney. It was to climax with a series of meetings in the Civic Centre at Hurstville. In preparation for these, I preached in as many of the local churches as would have me. I rang one of the ministers on the Saturday night before I was to preach for him. While there was no doubt about the fact that he was expecting me to come, I had an uneasy feeling that nothing had been done about inviting non-churchgoers to the service. So I said, 'You are expecting me to preach evangelistically, aren't you?' To which he replied, 'Is there any preaching which isn't evangelistic?'

I have pondered that often. The answer is of course both 'yes' and 'no'.

Is every sermon evangelistic?

To the question, 'What is the overall message of the Bible?' there might be many answers: it is a revelation of God's character; it is a record of the 'mighty deeds of God'. While these are true, they do no justice to the Bible's overriding theme. The Bible shows above all how God reconciles the world to himself in Christ.

When the risen Lord Jesus appeared to the two disciples on their way to Emmaus, he chided them for not understanding the fact that he, the Messiah, had to suffer before entering into his glory. ' "How foolish you are, and how slow of heart to believe all that the prophets have spoken! Did not the Christ have to suffer these things and then enter into his glory?" And beginning with Moses and all the Prophets, he explained to them what was said in all the Scriptures concerning himself' (Lk. 24:25–27).

Later that day, the risen Lord Jesus appeared to his disciples in the Upper Room. He commented:

'This is what I told you while I was still with you: Everything must be fulfilled that is written about me in the Law of

Moses, the Prophets and the Psalms.'
Then he opened their minds so they could understand the Scriptures . . . 'This is what is written: The Christ will suffer and rise from the dead on the third day, and repentance and forgiveness of sins will be preached in his name to all nations . . .' (Lk. 24:44–47)

It was by reference to the Old Testament Scriptures that Jesus chose to interpret the events of his life.
In a discussion with the Pharisees Jesus said:

'You diligently study the Scriptures because you think that by them you possess eternal life. These are the Scriptures that testify about me, yet you refuse to come to me to have life . . .
But do not think I will accuse you before the Father. Your accuser is Moses, on whom your hopes are set. If you believed Moses, you would believe me, for he wrote about me. But since you do not believe what he wrote, how are you going to believe what I say?' (Jn. 5:39–40, 45–47)

The Old Testament as well as the New has its focus on the Lord Jesus who is the centre of God's plans for the creation (Eph. 3:11). No doubt this is why Paul is able to say that the Scriptures (which for him would have been the Old Testament) are able to make us 'wise for salvation through faith in Christ Jesus' (2 Tim. 3:15).
When the Scriptures are seen as pointing us to salvation through faith in Christ, then, if dealt with in its context, any part of the Bible must be evangelistic. My observation is that most preachers know only that individual verses are to be understood in the immediate context of the particular book from which they come. Not everyone, however, seems to remember to place particular parts in their overall biblical context. When this is done, the sermon will be evangelistic, because it will show how this particular part fits into the whole revelation. If we cannot show how some part of the Bible fits into the overarching revelation of 'God reconciling the world to himself in Christ' (2 Cor. 5:19), there is a good chance that we have misunderstood it.
To expound the Old Testament as if Christ had not come does not do it justice. If a Jew (or even a Muslim) is happy with some exposition of the Old Testament, then it cannot be Christian in its interpretation.
What then do evangelists do when they are preaching? Is there anything distinctive in their sermons? It seems to me that they select parts of the Bible which summarize the great theme of redemption, such as John 3:16; 1 Corinthians 15:3ff.; and Isaiah 53:6ff. Because

these texts are such clear statements of the Bible's overall theme, they take us straight to the heart of the gospel.

What is the news which converts the world?

Good news is always worth telling. A friend of mine was so excited at the birth of his first child that he rushed out into the deserted car park at Bankstown Hospital at 3.00am and shouted at the top of his lungs, 'I'm a father!' Good news must be shared.

On the other hand, bad news has a stifling effect. No-one wants to bring bad news. More than thirty years ago, I was an assistant minister in a country town in New South Wales. A lad on holiday with a friend had been accidentally killed on a tractor on a sheep station. The owners asked me to take this news to his parents. How I wished I hadn't been at home! I wished the car wouldn't start. I hoped the parents wouldn't be at home when I arrived. I hoped anything which would prevent me being the bearer of such bad news.

Gospel preachers, however, are not like that. They have a wonderful message. It is summed up in those words spoken by the angels to herald the birth of Jesus: 'Today in the town of David a Saviour has been born to you; he is Christ the Lord' (Lk. 2:11). The message is of universal significance; it is good news of great joy for *all people*. It is about a rescue operation; the one who was born is a *Saviour*. It is about God's king (Messiah); *Christ the Lord*.

If Christ Jesus has come into the world to rescue us, from what do we need to be saved?

To answer this, we need to go back to the first book of the Bible, Genesis. This has the key which opens up to us how all the problems from which we need to be rescued began. At the end of chapter 1 we are told that God created the universe, our world; and he created people 'in his own image' (Gn. 1:26–27). In the second chapter marriage is instituted. The chapter ends with everything in harmonious relationship. The man and the woman are open with each other – nothing to hide. The couple are living in a harmonious relationship with God, and the world is a welcoming and agreeable environment. Everything in the garden was rosy. By the end of the third chapter, everything seems to have fallen apart. The man and the woman are threatened by each other. Because they fear exposure they 'hide' from each other; they wish they were not in this situation. They make clothes with fig leaves. Not very substantial! They hope they will soon be back to where they were before – open, loving and unashamed (Gn. 2:25). But time will show that they need a rescuer on a much bigger scale than they imagined.

When God comes to them we discover that they now feel threatened by him. When he calls, 'Where are you?' Adam replies, 'I was afraid because I was naked; so I hid' (Gn. 3:10). He wants to be found (or he would not have spoken), but he does not want to be revealed in his new disobedient condition. He feels threatened by God and needs to be rescued.

For the man and the woman, life becomes difficult. The environment in which they live now threatens them (Gn. 3:17–19). It is no longer the pleasant, all-providing garden. Death begins to set in as they grow old and no longer have access to the tree of life (Gn. 3:24). They need to be rescued from this.

Marriage is under threat. The man now wishes to dominate his wife; gone are mutual love, openness and respect (Gn. 3:16). They need to be rescued.

The cause of this tragedy needs to be identified and tackled. Remedial action is called for. The cause of the problem is easy to identify. The man and the woman have been tricked by the serpent into joining him in his rebellion against God (Gn. 3:1, 6). They have been duped into believing that they will be gods themselves, able to exercise their own rule and authority independently of God (Gn. 3:5). This proved to be a terrible lie. Even as God himself is pronouncing the just judgment on the man and the woman, however, he gives them hope. The offspring of the woman will crush Satan (Gn. 3:15). This 'offspring' turns out to be the Lord Jesus. If the man and the woman thought they had done a small thing, they were mistaken. What happened had devastating consequences as the whole human race lurched into further acts of disobedience towards God. This continued until Jesus, the Rescuer, was born. He, by his sinless life, sin-bearing death, and resurrection, dealt with the devil and rescued those who trust him. This is good news indeed.

How does God rescue the world?

'The reason the Son of God appeared was to destroy the devil's work' (1 Jn. 3:8) is how the apostle John summarizes Christ's work. Jesus destroyed the devil when he died and rose again for us. A way was opened for our release from bondage to Satan, sin and death. When the Lord Jesus died he took the punishment which our sins deserved (Mk. 10:45). The barrier between us and God is removed and we are acceptable to God and no longer threatened by him (Eph. 2:11–21). We can be at peace with him. This is very good news.

This action has a wonderful effect on the way we now can view each other. If I am acceptable to God through the work of Christ, then I must be acceptable to other Christians. If they are acceptable to God because of the work of Christ, they must be acceptable to me. There is no way that we could take up a different standard of acceptance. The fear of each other is removed in the death of Jesus. I do not need to be threatened by the possibility that someone will discover something in my past which disqualifies me. It has been dealt with in the death of the Lord Jesus. In Christian fellowship are love and acceptance. Christ breaks down the barriers between people, bringing them together in a new humility (Eph. 2:11–21). It is very good news indeed.

When Jesus rose from the dead he ushered in a new order for the creation. He is creating a new world in which those who are his will live for ever. The new world, unlike our present one, will not threaten us at all. This is how Isaiah describes it:

> The wolf will live with the lamb,
>   the leopard will lie down with the goat,
> the calf and the lion and the yearling together;
>   and a little child will lead them . . .
> They will neither harm nor destroy
>   on all my holy mountain . . .   (Is. 11:6, 9)

The apostle John describes it this way:

> 'Now the dwelling of God is with men, and he will live with them. They will be his people, and God himself will be with them and be their God. He will wipe every tear from their eyes. There will be no more death or mourning or crying or pain, for the old order of things has passed away.'
>
>   He who was seated on the throne said, 'I am making everything new!' (Rev. 21:3–5)

While I do not doubt for a moment that both these descriptions are poetic in style, they give us great confidence and hope as we await this final act of salvation. Jesus, through his death and resurrection, destroys the work of the devil and restores to his people everything that was lost through disobedience. It is a great message – so wonderful that it must be told.

The person who does this for us is Christ the Lord. He is king. Both John the Baptist and the Lord Jesus preached the gospel that 'the kingdom of God is near. Repent and believe the good news!' (Mk. 1:15). There is no doubt that Jesus saw that the kingdom had arrived in himself and that he was the strong man who had overpowered his and our enemies (Lk. 11:21–22).

In Luke's mind there is no difference between the gospel Jesus was preaching and the gospel Paul was preaching. Twice in the Acts of the Apostles, Paul's preaching is referred to as 'preaching the kingdom'. At

Miletus Paul uses the phrase to describe his preaching at Ephesus, and Luke uses it to describe Paul's work during his house arrest in Rome (Acts 20:25; 28:31).

The Bible defines the gospel in terms of Jesus: who he is and what he has come into the world to do. In Romans 1, God's gospel is described as 'the gospel ... regarding his Son' (Rom. 1:2–3). Whenever we are proclaiming the gospel it is the Lord Jesus we are talking about. The gospel does not originate with us, nor does it derive its content from us. It is not primarily about us and our needs (although these may well motivate us to listen; Jn. 4 gives us an example of this), but having done that, the gospel must focus on Jesus.

What response are we looking for in preaching?

When Paul reminds the elders from Ephesus about his ministry with them, he sums it up like this:

> 'You know that I have not hesitated to preach anything that would be helpful to you but have taught you publicly and from house to house. I have declared to both Jews and Greeks that they must turn to God in repentance and have faith in our Lord Jesus.' (Acts 20:20–21)

What the apostle did publicly he also did privately. In his mind there was no contradiction between preaching and pastoring. They were the same activity. Also, there was a sameness about the response he was seeking in his preaching. Whether it was Jew or Gentile, repentance and faith were the proper way to respond. It seems that when preaching to the Gentiles there was a different approach from that used when speaking to the Jews (Acts 17:16–34; *cf.* 13:16–41), yet the apostle was seeking to bring them *both* to repentance and faith. This is beautifully illustrated in the description of the response of the Thessalonians to the gospel: 'You turned to God from idols to serve the living and true God [repentance] and to wait for his Son from heaven, whom he raised from the dead – Jesus, who rescues us from the coming wrath [faith]' (1 Thes. 1:9–10).

Was Paul evangelizing all the time?

Are we to believe from Paul that he did this each time he preached? The answer is yes! In one form or another, whether the sermon was specifically evangelistic or teaching on the Christian life, there would have been a 'repentance and faith' component. The words themselves may not necessarily have been used, but the concepts would have been there nonetheless. Let me illustrate this with the parable of the persistent widow, which teaches that one 'should always pray and not give up' (Lk. 18:1–8). The main aim of a sermon on this passage is not evangelistic in the narrow sense, yet the preacher must urge hearers to repent of their failure to pray and remind them to put their faith in the God who hears and answers prayer. There must be a 'repentance and faith' component if preaching is to be directed to the will and not just to the mind or to the emotions. This repentance and faith, directed to a small area of the Christian life (namely prayer), are like the whole of the Christian response to the gospel. When we responded initially to the gospel, we repented of an existence independent of God. We acknowledged Jesus to be our Lord and we recognized that his lordship extended over every area of our lives. We also put our faith and trust in the fact that God would accept us because of the death and resurrection of the Lord Jesus. We trusted God to keep his promises.

The way we began is the way we continue. Paul describes it like this: 'So then, just as you received Christ Jesus as Lord, continue to live in him' (Col. 2:6). Therefore, it is unhelpful to suggest to Christian people that the gospel has become in some way unnecessary for them. I have heard ministers encourage them to bring their friends to evangelistic meetings by saying, 'Don't come if you haven't got a friend to bring', as if gospel preaching were good for unbelievers but somehow no longer helpful to believers. Gospel preaching is as good for us today as it was the first day we heard it.

I am not saying that a person gets converted over and over again. At our conversion we pledged our whole life to obey the Lord Jesus. We put our trust in God's reliability and trustworthiness, especially over the matter of our acceptability to him because of the work of Jesus. Subsequent repentance and faith 'renewals' are on specific issues of life over which we are either unaware or have become wilful in disobedience, so that appropriate action is necessary. We reapply the gospel to those specific areas of our lives because we have already committed it to the whole. It is rather like marriage vows and promises. They are absolute in commitment and are lived out day by day. When they are forgotten, with behaviour at odds with those commitments, an apology and changed behaviour are in order. Both relationships have a beginning and both have ongoing dynamic continuance. The continuation is on the basis of the beginning. This is further illustrated in the statement which introduces Paul's teaching about Christ's resurrection and ours: 'I want to remind you of the gospel I preached to you, which you received and on which you have taken your stand. By this gospel you are saved, if you hold firmly to the word I preached to you' (1 Cor. 15:1–2).

Preparing and preaching evangelistic sermons

This section will deal with some of the nuts and bolts of preparing and preaching evangelistic sermons.

Selecting the Bible passage

The first thing is to select the Bible passage for the sermon. The passage should enable us to proclaim the great work of God in reconciling the world to himself in Christ Jesus, and also to point people to repentance and faith. So I look for passages which show Jesus as Lord and Saviour. We preach him as Lord (to urge repentance), and as Saviour (to encourage faith).

An illustration can be seen in the incident when the Lord Jesus stills the storm at sea (Mk. 4:35–41). Here he is shown as Lord of the creation (see Ps. 89:9) as well as the Saviour of his disciples. He is able to rescue them because he is Lord. This passage is like an embryo of the whole gospel, and could legitimately be used to explain the whole gospel.

Another illustration is the passage in which Jesus cleanses the man suffering from leprosy (Mt. 8:1–4). The man is ceremonially unclean. He comes to Jesus, who touches him and heals him. Jesus, who is 'clean' in every way, now becomes 'unclean', having touched the man, who becomes clean again. It is like the whole gospel, and is a perfect illustration of 2 Corinthians 5:21: 'God made him who had no sin to be sin for us, so that in him we might become the righteousness of God.'

In many churches I attend, Bibles are provided. But many evangelistic talks and sermons are delivered where there are no Bibles – for instance, where I am an 'after-dinner speaker'. It is an easy matter to have the passage printed on to a place card so that people can have it in their hand and can see that what I am saying is what the Bible says. It is also easy to have the Bible passage printed on the 'pew notices' or on a separate handout. For those unfamiliar with the Bible, this can be less intimidating than being asked by the preacher to look up some part of it.

Understanding the passage

There is no real difference between preparing the evangelistic sermon and preparing any other sermon. What varies is the content. The aim of the evangelistic sermon is always narrow: to bring people to repentance and faith by presenting the gospel, that is, Jesus. The usual exegetical skills are brought into play; we do not impose on to the text ideas which God never intended to be there. The evangelistic sermon needs to be simple and easy to follow, but this does not exempt us from the work of making sure we understand the meaning of the passage. It

174

may, in fact, require *more* care. The usual questions should be asked: What does the passage say? What do the words mean? What do they mean in their context? What do they mean in the context of the whole Bible? What kind of literature is it? Why did the writer say it at all? Why did the writer say it like this? What did the original readers think it meant?

Having understood the passage, we are now in a position to lay out the shape or structure of the sermon.

Structure

The aim of evangelistic preaching, proclaiming Jesus as Lord and Saviour, will dictate the major points to be made during the sermon. These will be selected from the material gathered while working at understanding the passage. When we have selected the major points, we are in a position to 'flesh out' the sermon. For several years I have followed a formula to do this.

1. *State the point.* Put it to the hearers as clearly and as simply as you can.

2. *Explain the point.* Tell them what it means, explain the context, and show that this is what the passage says.

3. *Illustrate the point.* Give an example of the importance of the point you are making. Illustrate it with a story or some other part of the Bible.

4. *Apply the point.* Suggest to the hearers how they should respond now to this part of the Bible, and urge them to do so.

Introduction, illustration and conclusion

Having done the body of the sermon, we need to work on the *introduction*. Here we are trying to discover what we can say which will cause people to want to listen to the rest of the sermon! Therefore, while the introduction should take a very short time to deliver, it is very important. It should arouse attention and touch a point of interest or need in the hearer. This could be done by asking a question to which the rest of the sermon is the answer. A problem can be stated and answered by the sermon. This is easier said than done! It takes me a great deal of time to work on this very important step in preparation. During the course of preparing and practising any given sermon I might try several different introductions.

Many sermons begin by using an *illustration*. The story is often intriguing, but I think the full impact is wasted when the hearers do not yet know its point. It would be better left until they know what point it is illustrating.

When I have finished the introduction I want the hearers to say in their minds something like: 'I'm glad I didn't stay in bed. This is exactly what I want to hear', or 'That's a great question; I want to know the answer to that.'

Many non-churchgoers are unused to listening to anyone for any length of time. Consequently the use of *stories and illustrations* is very important in evangelistic preaching. When illustrations are used well, they help to clarify and reinforce points already made. As well as this, they often give the listener time to relax; the same degree of concentration is not needed to listen to a story. They often regain lapsed attention.

Stories do, however, have limitations. When the story is so vivid that people remember it but not the point it is illustrating, it is self-defeating. Inaccurate illustrations can be distracting, as people are sidetracked into thinking about it. Stories that do not in fact illustrate the point are confusing. Some people who may have understood the original points might now be rendered quite uncertain of them.

The *conclusion* is directed towards a person's will. We are looking for people to take action. Note how Paul spoke about his preaching: 'We implore you on Christ's behalf: Be reconciled to God' (2 Cor. 5:20). 'We proclaim him, admonishing and teaching everyone with all wisdom' (Col. 1:28). Paul aimed, through the Spirit, by means of the Word of God, to change people. His appeal was to the will. It is possible to preach to the mind, and people will be stimulated. It is possible to preach to the heart, and the emotions will be stirred. On both occasions people will speak encouragingly of how effective they found such preaching. But it will have no lasting value unless it is directed to the will.

Never is this more so than in evangelistic preaching. We are preaching with the aim that men and women will respond with repentance and faith. Such decisions are made not by the mind or by the emotions, although both will be involved. They are made by the will. Those famous words, 'I will', used in the marriage promises, are very appropriate in evangelism. Through the mind and the emotions we are seeking to persuade people that the Word of God should be taken seriously, so this must be apparent to them. It is a matter of life and death! We are not asking them to sign up for a new hobby course. We are offering forgiveness of sins, a place in heaven. We are warning them of the horror of judgment and hell. Tears would be appropriate (Acts 20:19). Our preaching on these issues cannot be matter-of-fact, as if the outcome did not really matter, but must be delivered with passion. The conclusion of the sermon should give clear directions on how people should respond appropriately. The concluding prayer is an excellent point at which to direct people to turn to God, and can be phrased in such language that people who pray and mean it will truly turn to Christ by means of it.

Having concluded the preparations, we now need to practise the sermon until we are conversant with the material and can deliver it confidently. I do not want to give the impression, however, that the activity of evangelistic preaching is mechanical or that it should be engaged in without prayer or without being mindful of the spiritual warfare in which we are engaged.

Prayer and evangelistic preaching

Prayer plays an important and integral part in evangelistic preaching. Prayer takes place during preparation, that God's Spirit will help us to understand the passage properly and teach it in such a way as truly to say what it 'says'. During this time I also pray for the hearers, so that they will be prepared by God to receive the message. It is while I am preaching, however, that I am most at prayer. I am constantly praying that God will open 'blind eyes' to the truth set before them. I am directing my preaching to the hearers' will, but I know that unless God graciously intervenes and changes their will, nothing will truly happen. This truth is taught consistently in the Scriptures (*e.g.* Mt. 11:25–27; Jn. 3:1–8; 6:44; 2 Cor. 4:1–6), and it causes me to stay at prayer during the preaching. It wonderfully releases the preacher from having to obtain results. They, mercifully, are in the hands of God. He can be trusted to do his work well.

Spiritual warfare and evangelistic preaching

The whole Christian life can be depicted as warfare. Paul does this in Ephesians 6 and urges us to take appropriate action. In evangelistic preaching I have experienced this spiritual warfare in two particular areas. The first comes when I see the congregation: 'There are no outsiders here. You can tell at a glance.' This is completely irrational. As an itinerant I don't know them at all. Even if I did, I certainly do not know the state of their standing before God. Thus I am tempted to be discouraged from proclaiming the gospel before I even start. This thinking has its origin in the 'pit', and is to be resisted.

The second is at the end of the sermon when I am appealing to people to turn to Christ. It never seems 'right' to ask them to do it *now*. If I were to follow my feelings at this moment, I would never do it. I think this is part of the spiritual warfare. I should resist the devil in this matter (Jas. 4:7). I have given them the information necessary to act. I have presented this material in an appealling way. I have been praying that God will open 'blind eyes'. Appealling to them to turn to Christ is the most obvious thing to do. So I do it against my feelings!

Expectations and evangelistic preaching

I wish to conclude this essay where I began, with a reminder that the gospel is 'the power of God for the salvation of everyone who believes' (Rom. 1:16). When you preach evangelistically, what is *your* expectation? Do you think people will be converted and turn to Christ for mercy?

Many years ago I was staying with Dick Lucas at the Rectory in Bishopsgate. He had kindly invited me to preach at the lunchtime services on Tuesdays at St Helen's. The sermons were teaching-evangelism. The attendances were large. After each service, people would introduce me to their friends who were attending *for the first time*. There were not a few. It caused me to reflect. Why did these people continue week after week to bring new friends along? Because they had confidence in the preaching of the gospel to change their friends' lives! They were not ashamed of the gospel. They believed that it was the power of God for the salvation of everyone who believed. It had a profound effect on me. It made me question my own expectation, and renew my faith in the preaching of the gospel. I believe there was a noticeable change in the way I preached. It was best described as 'calmly confident'.

The gospel will do its work. There is preaching which can 'convert the world'!

Let the apostle Paul have the last word:

> Preach the Word; be prepared in season and out of season; correct, rebuke and encourage – with great patience and careful instruction . . . But you, keep your head in all situations, endure hardship, do the work of an evangelist, discharge all the duties of your ministry. (2 Tim. 4:2, 5)

12

Preparing the preacher

David Jackman

The present situation

There can be little doubt that the effective selection, training and deployment of a new generation of gospel ministers constitute one of the greatest unsung needs of the contemporary evangelical church. This is true across the denominations, irrespective of structures, roles and titles, and whether the ministry is full-time or part-time. Many local congregations are crying out for mature and visionary leadership. They have often sunk into 'maintenance mode', discouraged by the sheer enormity of their task and the hostility of the climate, resigned to keeping the doors open and the roof on, together with providing a bare minimum of services, as the most that anyone can legitimately expect. Nor can any of us afford to be negatively critical of this situation. Local church ministry in the Protestant West is increasingly tough, whether one is facing the rootless impersonality of the inner city, coping with the peripatetic demands of running half a dozen rural parishes, or trying to achieve change in an evangelical congregation which has become wedded to its hallowed traditions rather than to the radical demands of Scripture.

Not surprisingly, the last thirty years have seen a multitude of 'solutions' offering to fill the vacuum and turn matters around. Many of them have included excellent elements – training in personal evangelism, church-growth theory with its practical insights, the development of house-groups – while others have promised more than they have been able to deliver. But the tide has not yet turned, and it is arguable that although Sunday attendance at church has generally remained static, or has even slightly improved, the coming generations demonstrate less knowledge of the faith, fewer connections with the church and more widespread unbelief than for decades, if not for centuries. The task facing us is enormous.

The reasons for all this are not too difficult to discover, and analyses abound. We are reaping the harvest of intellectual atheism that has been sown in our universities throughout the century. Scientific determinism, atheistic humanism and destructive liberal criticism of the Bible have all combined to undermine *any* ultimate authority (let alone the Bible), and with it any confidence about the purpose of human existence. As this has trickled through our mass communications, it has also profoundly affected Christian thinking. We have seen a century of defection from organized Christianity and an emptying of the churches in the West. In more recent years, the development of deconstructionism has meant, at the popular level, that there need no longer be any attempt to strive for meaning. The only truth that exists is what I decide is reality for me, whether or not anyone else agrees with me, or is even interested. It is a heady recipe for personal freedom, restricted only by a tolerant social convention, which is all the time itself being eroded.

Into this climate, the Christian preacher comes with claims about absolute truth, a God whose unchanging character is expressed in eternal laws, real moral guilt before a really holy God, and the need of forgiveness. In addition, he speaks about a God who becomes human in order to suffer and die to redeem us, about heaven and hell, and about the resurrection of the body and the life everlasting. We would be very shortsighted to underestimate the totally alien nature of this message to our contemporaries, as the twentieth century draws to its close.

So what are we to do? The church has been grappling with that question for most of the century, and has come up with two main solutions. The first has been to change the message, in order to make it more understandable and palatable to contemporary tastes. The examples are legion. A recent one concerns the 'sacking' of a young Anglican vicar, in the diocese of Chichester, by his bishop. No longer believing in God as an objective reality, but rather as a projection of all that he most values within his humanity, he has been deprived of his living – to the outrage of the media. To them, this is another example of the church alienating those who similarly cannot believe in the traditional Christian God, but who might otherwise 'support' the church. Rather like a football club, the church exists as a focus for its supporters' dreams. Evangelicals are very familiar with this reductionism, and rightly have a long and honourable history of resisting it.

By contrast, the evangelical response has often been to carry on as though nothing has changed. In many of our buildings very little has changed, and it is increasingly difficult, if they are listed, to see how much, if anything, can change. On this view, for many members of the general public, the churches are an extension of the National Trust. The services are either quaintly antiquarian in musical form and liturgy, or culturally restricted to the current jargon and fashionable style of a particular social grouping of insiders. A great deal of church time is still spent on servicing ourselves, as though we had no problems in building bridges to outsiders. Much of our evangelism is directed at people who are already on the Christian fringe. But if the trend is to be reversed, we shall have to start reaching those who are beyond the present orbit of any of our churches. This will require huge outlays of energy and time, which at present we seem too under-resourced to offer. So we all tend to look for the quick fix.

Like many others, I have been impressed and challenged by the evangelistic philosophy and practice of Willow Creek Community Church in Barrington, Illinois, under the visionary and gifted leadership of its pastor, Bill Hybels. We have been learning again that 'lost people matter to God', and that if they matter so much to him they must become our priority too. Church is for the 'unchurched'. But as the news of Willow Creek has spread through its conferences, videos and seminars, it has been fascinating to see how church leaders around the world have tried to reproduce elements of Willow Creek with very little cultural adaptation. This has led to criticism of Willow Creek's methodology – although Bill Hybels consistently warns us not to do what they do, but to ask the questions they have asked so as to come to our own authentic, culturally appropriate answers. That takes time, prayer, study, and listening – and time is what most of us do not have, or will not make. We would rather carry on 'doing church' the way we always have, with a bit of updating and including a modified form of the newest evangelical fashions to keep the insiders happy. This 'add-on' procedure is never going to change the surrounding culture; it merely apes it. But the Christian ghetto that does not or cannot build meaningful relationships with unchurched people will never change the surrounding culture either.

Identifying the problem

What is going wrong? Are we just failing to produce young people of ability and enthusiasm in their commitment to the Lord and the gospel? That does not seem to be the case, given the strength of the Christian witness in our universities, or the extensive summer camps and house parties of many splendid evangelical organizations. There are many keen and able young believers who are not ashamed of the gospel and who are prepared to devote time and energy sacrificially to serve Christ. Can they not communicate effectively to their peer group? Apparently, many can and do, though inevitably some are less confident and more introverted. Why, then, do we not see these enthusiasms and skills being developed and put to use in effective church leadership? Why do so many of even the new churches complain of a leadership vacuum among the twentysomethings and thirtysomethings? Undoubtedly some do fall away, as the parable of the soils leads us to expect. The worries of life, along with its riches and pleasures, all play their part in choking the good seed as time passes (Lk. 8:14). But that is not the whole story, or even the major part of it. Many keen young Christians start to train for ministry only to find their spiritual edge blunted, their convictions deflated and the overwhelming pressure of academic correctness gradually stifling their zeal and enthusiasm. They have become professionals, products of the church-worker production line, except that the design no longer meets the needs of the changed market, and much of what has been produced is redundant. Many young ministers soon discover themselves to be under-equipped for ministry.

I once heard a young trainee minister interviewed in church, at the end of his first year. Asked what he had learned in that year of training, he replied, 'Well, just that we don't have many answers.' The academic agenda of the secular universities' departments of theology has shaped the syllabus of many ministry training colleges in an alarming way. The academic tail wags the ministry dog so energetically that many congregations discover that the keen young people they sent off for training come back less well equipped for the real job than when they first left them. They are able to write essays to explore the higher reaches of fashionable theological speculation, but not to use the Bible with confidence in a way that actually nurtures the flock, whether by public preaching or private pastoring.

Please do not misread me. I am not writing off theological study and intellectual endeavour of the most rigorous kind, nor am I saying that colleges and seminaries are unimportant – far from it. But if we were to give ourselves the leisure to stand back and ask what sort of training we would need to put in place in order to produce a steady flow of competent ministers for the challenging, contemporary context we have outlined, we would have to acknowledge that the changes would have to be deep. The urgency of the hour is such that all of us who have any real concern for the future ministry of the church ought to see the exercise as a necessity, not a luxury, demanding radical action. Of course, as biblical evangelicals, we shall come up with very different answers from those whose theological authority base varies from ours. Our views of the ministry (as of the church, and as indeed of the gospel) will be radically different, due to our different presuppositions about ultimate authority. This is not the place to argue these issues, only to comment that a theological training in which they become the major focus is bound to send out its students less equipped for ministry in practical terms (though arguably some may be rather sharper theologically).

The solution in Scripture

It is time to dream our dream. What sort of training do we need to see established, if we are to produce able ministers of the new covenant who will impact the culture of the twenty-first century, and set in place gospel work that is constantly bearing fruit and growing? True to our evangelical roots, we need to take ourselves first to Scripture and to a study of ministry in the New Testament, in order to determine the Holy Spirit's priorities as expressed through and by the apostles.

In this short compass, we can only summarize a rich biblical seam by quoting from Paul's last letter, his second to Timothy. Knowing that the time for his departure had come, and standing on the time-line between the apostolic and post-apostolic church, Paul's great concern is for both purity of sound doctrine and zeal in gospel work. In the face of mounting clouds of persecution, he wants the church to hold firm to the faith and to keep proclaiming the gospel whatever the cost. 2 Timothy is full of it. 'Fan into flame the gift of God, which is in you' (1:6). 'Do not be ashamed to testify about our Lord . . . But join with me in suffering for the gospel' (1:8). 'Keep . . . the pattern of sound teaching' (1:13). 'Guard the good deposit that was entrusted to you' (1:14). 'And the things you have heard me say in the presence of many witnesses entrust to reliable men who will also be qualified to teach others' (2:2). 'Do your best to present yourself to God as one approved, a workman who does not need to be ashamed and who correctly handles the word of truth' (2:15). And so it proceeds, until the great and solemn climax is reached. 'In the presence of God and of Christ Jesus, who will judge the living and the dead, and in view of his appearing and his kingdom, I give you this charge: Preach the Word; be prepared in season and out of season; correct, rebuke and encourage –

with great patience and careful instruction' (4:1–2). Search as we may, we find nothing here about a sacramental, priestly ministry, or one of signs and wonders. It is all about ministry of the Word as the church moves from the certainty of apostolic inspiration into an unknown and dangerous future, when the generation of eyewitnesses has passed on to heaven and the church on earth still awaits the King's parousia. Without an effective ministry of the Word in the congregation, there cannot be a strong and effective ministering church in the world.

Today, this is being increasingly recognized across the evangelical spectrum. In his recent book *Mighty Manifestations*, Reinhard Bonnke writes in the introduction, 'I decided that for us our grounds must be the Word and that is where we stand. This meant that our entire "pneumatology" (the things of the Spirit) had to be subjected to the judgement of "what the Word says" . . . The challenge to experience must come from Scripture. Experience must not challenge Scripture nor adapt Scripture to what "happens to happen".[1] Unless there is a commonly agreed authority, there can be no forward movement. The full-time Christian minister must be both governed by, and a servant of, the Word (Lk. 1:2).

The first ingredient in our training for ministry must therefore be the Word of God – the Bible, the whole Bible and nothing but the Bible, in the sense that its own message is far more important than all the libraries of speculative scholarship on matters of introduction and textual criticism. Yet most academic courses spend far more time in the secondary literature than in the primary text. Part of the problem here is that of the biblical languages, which modern students with little knowledge of grammar (of any sort) find increasingly hard to master. We all know that many very effective preachers have 'little Greek and less Hebrew', and that the languages are not essential for expository preaching, since so many reliable textual commentaries exist. But it is also true that the preacher who is at least 'lexicon-literate', and who has some feel for the structures and rhythms of the biblical languages, will usually handle the text more ably and with greater confidence in seeking to understand and convey accurately its meaning to the contemporary congregation.

The last part of that sentence is of vital importance. For although Scripture is God's timeless and universal Word, it is also set in historical particularity. One may make the same point another way, by affirming that although the Holy Spirit is the author and generator of Scripture, he chose to use human writers and historical events as the channel of that revelation. If this is the 'given' of God's self-revelation, then clearly it provides a pattern which must be reflected in any Word ministry. We cannot simply draw a line from the biblical text to the contemporary preacher and his congregation without engaging in a hermeneutic which must take us to the original context, so that we may hear its message 'as originally given', as authentically and meaningfully as possible. This will require the discipline of examining and understanding each text in its own context, within the argument or narrative or oracle of which it is a part, within the book to which it belongs and within the development of the whole revelation of biblical theology or salvation-history.

The Word in the world

Clearly, many of the traditional ingredients of theological education are vital to this task. Languages, exegesis, hermeneutics and systematics all have their vital role to play. But the preacher, as distinct from the scholar, has a further road to travel. Recognizing that we shall not begin to understand and apply God's unchanging Word correctly to our generation unless we can first follow through the same process with regard to the original hearers or readers, he has nevertheless to convey those 'timeless truths' with contemporary acuity. Only then will the Word of God, which is 'living and active' and 'sharper than any double-edged sword', do its designated work of penetrating, dividing and judging 'the thoughts and attitudes of the heart' (Heb. 4:12). The issue of how this should or can be done, in practice, provides us with what is arguably the most important watershed in current evangelism.

In recent years, a gulf has opened up between the great objective truths of the biblical revelation (orthodox Christian believing) and the deeply felt, subjective needs and experience of the Christian believer. This is expressed in a variety of ways, usually by a set of profoundly unhelpful and unbiblical antitheses. So the 'Word-Christian' is characterized by an emphasis on the truth, the mind and doctrine, while the 'Spirit-Christian', by contrast, emphasizes the spirit, the heart and experience. The smear words are, respectively, 'cerebral' and 'emotional'. But these are not just 'positions'; they open up widely differing versions of evangelical Christianity. In an article in *Christianity Today*, introducing his book *Consulting the Faithful*, Richard Mouw, President of Fuller Theological Seminary in Pasadena, puts it like this:

> Many theologians today are suspicious of, and perhaps even hostile to, more popular expressions of the faith. Many evangelical scholars these days are publicly worrying about, for example, the popularity of recovery groups, Christian therapy centres, church-growth workshops, seminars in managerial methods for ministers, 'signs and wonders' movements, and 'power evangelism' strategies.

Mouw's point is that theological teachers and pastors should not label these developments as 'bad theology', but 'explore the deep spiritual yearnings at work in the grass-roots desire for visible and practical signs of God's presence'. They should be an important starting-point for theological reflection, affirming 'their vitality without endorsing them as adequate features of mature Christianity'.[2]

As always, we must look not for a balance between two extremes but for the biblical perpendicular. Examining the ends of the spectrum first, it is not difficult to see how orthodox Reformed theology *can* degenerate into an academicism in which the primary focus of interest is antiquarian. Knowledge of the truth can become a primary intellectual concern, and the battles with old heresies are then re-fought, using the language and thought forms of past eras. This can have a particular attraction for the quieter, more introverted personality, to whom the solitude of the library will always be more conducive than the babble of the market-place. It is rather like those historical societies which dress up to re-enact the battles of the Civil War. But the opposite end of the spectrum can be so culture-dominated that the church simply adds on the latest fads and fancies to an already need-centred spirituality. This is another form of self-indulgence, where almost anything contemporary can be baptized, so that the radical challenge of the gospel is lost in a thousand cultural qualifications of its demands. 'If it feels good, it must be of God' becomes the motto – and we have plenty of examples of where that road ends. I am not suggesting that either end of the spectrum is overcrowded, but it helps to clarify our thinking by identifying the extremes. The question then is, where is the perpendicular?

The biblical preacher must live in both the Word and the real world. But they are not to be of equal importance to him. The almost monastic separation of some training colleges, away from the city, separated from the living church, turned in on themselves, is no model to follow if we want to equip ministers who live in both locations. Actually, it models the wrong concept of holiness through withdrawal, which Jesus certainly did not practise with his own disciples. Perhaps financial constraints on this sort of unnecessary luxury will remove the larger part of theological training from the retreat model back to the involvement model, where the trainee is learning in the local congregation, testing and applying insights from study in the context of real-life ministry. The church has to live in the world and so have its pastor-teachers. But we are not to be dazzled or deceived by the world. 'Our citizenship is in heaven' (Phil. 3:20), and so we know that 'the world and its desires pass away, but the man who does the will of God lives for ever' (1 Jn. 2:17).

Our task, then, is not to listen to the world, in the sense of allowing it to set the agenda for the church, but to allow the Word to teach us what we need to know about the world, and then to apply its truth to the cultural particularity in which we are called to live. The culture may make many demands which have to be resisted, because 'we know that the whole world is under the control of the evil one' (1 Jn. 5:19). The culture may ask many questions which are not ultimately of significance at all. But it is only as we take those questions to Scripture that we find God redirecting our thinking and teaching us the real questions we need to ask if we are to engage with eternal realities. This is hard and demanding work. It is also dangerous, because the church is always much more likely to be influenced and infected by the culture in which it is planted than we care to admit. But we are called to minister to real people, to proclaim God's Word in Scripture as it is, his 'now' Word for today's people. We cannot do that at arm's length, or by hit-and-run raids.

The biblical example of Lot and his wife may help to make the point. Whatever we may think of the selfishness of Lot's choice of 'the whole plain of the Jordan . . . well watered, like the garden of the LORD' (Gn. 3:10), he had to live in a culture that was in flagrant rebellion against God. But 2 Peter 2:7–8 tells us that Lot was 'a righteous man . . . distressed by the filthy lives of lawless men' and 'tormented in his righteous soul by the lawless deeds he saw and heard'. It was God who rescued Lot, as he is able to rescue godly men from trials, Peter affirms. But Christ reminds us to 'remember Lot's wife!' (Lk. 17:32). It is possible to be so committed to the culture that its magnetic attraction overcomes the commands of God, with disastrous results. Indeed, that is the way we shall automatically go, unless we listen constantly to God's Word and judge our culture by its teaching.

Priorities in training

All this serves to underline how important it is to give time and thought to providing biblical priorities for the training of the next generation of pastor-teachers, whose role it is to equip the people of God to minister (Eph. 4:11–12). We must allow neither our traditions nor financial considerations to be the controlling factor. As we face the increasing secularization of our culture, but with it the increasingly unsatisfied spiritual appetites of men and women made in God's image, and restless without him, we have to ask; what sort of individual Christians and church communities do we need to pray and work for, to meet these immense challenges and needs? But we cannot stop there. We must go on to ask: what sort of servants (*diakonoi*) are needed to meet these needs? What sort of training is going to produce them?

Clearly we live in an age of spiritual hunger, because there is a famine of the Word of God. Although we have more aids to help us in Bible study than any previous generation, all the signs are that the Bible is studied less. Personal devotions, where they exist, have little biblical content, and, in much pulpit preaching, the Bible merely serves as a peg for the preacher to hang his hat on. It is nodded to, and used, but only comparatively rarely is it carefully expounded and thoroughly applied. There are outstanding exceptions, of which Dick Lucas' ministry, both at St Helen's and through the Proclamation Trust, is a glowing example. But the purpose of this book has been to argue for a return to serious Bible study, understanding, application and effective communication as the heart of the Christian ministry. Where the Bible is properly preached and taught, God's voice is heard, and where his voice is heard, sinners are saved, Christians develop in godliness and churches grow. The connection is not a coincidence.

We must re-establish the properly rigorous study of the Word of God at the heart of the training process, in place of the practice of 'adding on' which makes the minister a dabbler in pop psychology, managerial techniques or liturgical dance. Many traditional ingredients will have their part to play, such as church history and philosophy for apologetics. But nothing must be taught for its own sake, and few necessary ingredients should be taught by the traditional lecture methods alone. The ready availability of all the factual information any student is ever likely to need means that instruction time can increasingly be given to discussion, interaction, developing practical problem-solving and communication skills, in a hands-on, learning-by-doing style. This needs to be combined with the practical experience of real ministry in a variety of forms, carefully supervised and assessed, in the local church, on a continuous basis. The short placement of a month or so, in which a student hardly has time to get to know anyone, is singularly frustrating and ineffective for all concerned.

The goal of training for effective practical ministry, rather than for short-term academic achievement, will profoundly affect the Bible work done. We must call a halt to the worldliness that is simply interested in paper qualifications. We all know from our schooldays that some of our teachers with the best academic qualifications were actually the worst teachers. They had few relational skills and even less idea of the difficulties with the subject which their pupils faced. We cannot afford to perpetuate that model. It is the height of folly to select for ministry recluses who do not enjoy relating to people, on the grounds of their academic ability. It is equally foolish to expect those who have no appetite for study to be able to preach and tell the Word.

But if we reject the ministry as an ecclesiastical career, and see its role in terms of shepherding the flock by providing pasture and water, care and discipline, we understand immediately how important a correct and able handling of Scripture becomes. It is to be studied now, not as a detached subject of academic enquiry, but in order that the apprentice shepherd may himself be taught, rebuked, corrected and trained in righteousness, 'thoroughly equipped for every good work' (2 Tim. 3:16–17). That is the only way to produce a man or woman of God. We learn Scripture first in order to obey it, not to argue over it. And then we learn it to teach it to our fellow believers as powerfully and helpfully as we are able. So the learning is always to be undertaken with a view to doing and teaching, rather than simply remembering and reproducing.

This will mean spending time on the different genres of biblical literature, seeing how they are put together and working hard on their meaning and continuing message. Matters of date and authorship, along with a host of other critical questions, will become less important. They will often be useful to stimulate a fresh awareness of the range of issues raised by the text and to drive the student back to the text to examine it more carefully, but always with the primary purpose of obedience to God's infallible Word. As the different genres are encountered and studied, Scripture needs to be compared with Scripture, and the specific related to the 'big picture' of God's unfolding, progressive revelation through the whole Bible. This will require time to be spent on systematics, and especially on biblical theology. Not only the time-line of the Bible will need to be known, but also its great unifying themes, so that the trainee preacher can have confidence in relating the particular to the general, and see the development of God's great purpose for humankind from Genesis to Revelation. This will restore a sense of the unity and coherence of Scripture, and therefore develop a greater confidence in its reliability and value.

It will also help to counteract the unhealthy separation of the biblical revelation into Old and New Testaments, almost as though they were watertight compartments, which has done so much to divide Scripture from Scripture and undermine many a student's confidence in handling its so-called 'contradictions'. Obviously, time and careful study need to be given to these difficult questions, and there can be no sweeping the difficulties under the carpet. But they will be approached not from the sceptical presuppositions of destructive rationalism, but from the expectation of harmonization and unity, knowing that the same divine mind inspired each of the Bible authors. If we seem to find contradictions, they are going to stem from our deficient under-standing, rather than from any deficiency in God's communication. The likelihood that we are right and Scripture is wrong is as great as the likelihood that a stream will flow uphill, to use C. S. Lewis's analogy.

In our study of systematics, we will concentrate on the practical, pastoral value of the doctrine that is being understood. With many excellent handbooks available, we should be able to focus more time on the relevance and application of systematized truth to the life of the believer. We want to teach theology not as slabs of facts to be learned, but as the living truth of God to be applied to life. Theology classes could spend more time profitably discussing typical pastoral situations, and, like skilled medical students on a ward round, applying the knowledge gained to the patient's need. There will be no shortages of examples if the students are involved at the same time in practical ministry experience. That in turn stimulates a practical use of the Bible in pastoral theology, so that students begin to feel increasingly more able to apply truth to life, not only analytically, but with life-changing power.

Running through it all will be the central concern to preach the Word. I am not a great believer in homiletical models. Textbooks on the subject tend to be overly complex and technical, and their effect is to stultify or paralyse the natural ability an individual has. No-one can make a preacher out of someone who lacks the ability to communicate, but that is not so rare a gift, and I am convinced that many more quality preachers could be produced if we were to set our minds to the task. I know that the prevailing orthodoxy is that preaching is an outmoded and inefficient means of communication. I also know that boring and irrelevant pulpiteering is positively counterproductive. But churches are still being filled where the Bible is taught properly, and none of the alternatives is as cost-effective, or as successful, in growing strong disciples. Much of the hostility to preaching in the last twenty years or so simply reflects the culture's rejection of absolutes, and indeed all forms of authority. 'Preachy' is a highly pejorative term. Preaching is being rehabilitated, however, by improving its content and quality. The truth still needs to be taught, and, where that is done with honesty, authority, relevance and humility, it is powerfully effective. The day of the star preacher or orator may well be past (and that is probably a blessing), but every church needs a team of teacher-preachers, who correctly handle the Word of truth. In this, of course, the ministry of those who are not full-time or ordained will rightly increase in importance in the coming years.

In trying to teach people to preach, we want to develop their own natural talents and at all costs to avoid cloning. Some practical help on breathing, articulation and body-language is valuable, but the preacher · must not develop the wrong sort of self-consciousness. As much personal help as possible between tutor and student is of prime value. Fellow students also provide a valuable sounding-board. Honest criticism, *lovingly delivered*, is essential for an individual's development. Was there a clear message, and was it true to the biblical text? Did the structure help or hinder? (*Was* there a structure?) What was the sermon's theme (in a sentence) and what was its aim? Were both communicated? What did the sermon send its hearers away to believe, and to do? How helpful were the applications, and how useful the illustrations, if any? In this context, a student can experiment with different approaches and target congregations, different ways of presenting notes or working without them, knowing that the feedback will be both informed and supportive.

The call and the task

This has been the burden of the Proclamation Trust and especially of the Cornhill Training Course, during their few years of existence. They are the natural fruit of Dick Lucas' lifetime of Word ministry, which this volume honours in thanksgiving to God. There is nothing new about all this, though the context in which the unchanging principles have to be applied has probably never been more fluid. But Christians have always had to keep their nerve and their biblical cutting edge, in a world where hostility to God and to the gospel is the norm. Dick's own life is an outstanding example of that sort of biblical single-mindedness. It enables us to give thanks and to take courage in the same God for the future. In training a new generation of pastor-teachers, we would want to call one another to be faithful to Paul's concluding words to Timothy. 'But you, keep your head in all situations, endure hardship, do the work of an evangelist, discharge all the duties of your ministry' (2 Tim. 4:5). There can be no more important and no more urgent task.

Notes

1. Reinhard Bonnke, *Mighty Manifestations* (Eastbourne: Kingsway, 1984), p. 8.
2. *Christianity Today*, 18 July 1994.